THE SMART GUIDE

Horses and Riding

BY DEAN SERVER

SECOND EDITION

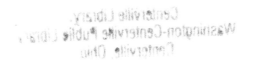

The Smart Guide To Horses and Riding

Published by

Smart Guide Publications, Inc.
2517 Deer Chase Drive
Norman, OK 73071
www.smartguidepublications.com

For information, address: Smart Guide Publications, Inc. 2517 Deer Creek Drive, Norman, OK 73071

SMART GUIDE and Design are registered trademarks licensed to Smart Guide Publications, Inc.

International Standard Book Number: 978-1-937636-74-6

Library of Congress Catalog Card Number:
11 12 13 14 15 10 9 8 7 6 5 4 3 2 1

Printed in the United States of America

Cover design: Lorna Llewellyn
Copy Editor: Ruth Strother
Back cover design: Joel Friedlander, Eric Gelb, Deon Seifert
Back cover copy: Eric Gelb, Deon Seifert
Illustrations: Carolyn Janik
Production: Zoë Lonergan
Indexer: Cory Emberson
V.P./Business Manager: Cathy Barker

ACKNOWLEDGMENTS

Completion of this book would not have happened without the help and support of industry friends Terri Hardin and her husband Lee. I would also like to thank Soojin Paik for her aid in this project as well as Thomas Jeffries for his kind assistance.

I would like to salute the public library of Lakewood, New Jersey for the use of their resources and for their patience during the research and assembly of this book. I should also thank Jean Mikle for her part in giving me the encouragement that helped make this book possible.

I would like to thank Ruth Strouther for her contribution to this book as my editor, to Cory Emberson for her careful proofreading and to James Balkovek for his wonderful illustrations.

TABLE OF CONTENTS

INTRODUCTION

Riding a horse can be a great joy, but not everyone who wants to ride knows how to get started. There are other folks who have started to ride or may have been riding a long time but still want to learn more.

This book will show you how to get started and will also explain tell you all you need to know about horses and riding. You'll also find out how to take care of them horses and what special needs they have.

You'll that the more you find out about horses and the more you're around horses, the more you'll like them. They are regal, powerful animals, but most of them are quite friendly. As you discover more about them, you'll understand why they've been loved and appreciated since pre-historic times.

This book will tell you all you need to know about how to find a horse to ride and what to do if you want to buy a horse or even buy a stable. You'll find out how to ride and how to take care of your horse. You'll find out what equipment you'll need to ride and how to take care of it.

Whatever your level of riding, from beginner to advanced, this volume will give you the information you want and need to become a capable rider and horse person.

PART ONE

History of the Horse and Its Breeds

CHAPTER 1

Evolution and History

> ## In This Chapter
>
> ➤ In the beginning
>
> ➤ Horses at work
>
> ➤ Horses in war

Fifty million years of evolution has turned a small creature that was about the size of a household cat into the modern horse. In this chapter, you'll learn all about the development of the species and how it evolved into the animal we now know and love.

You'll also learn about people's first known connection with the horse and some of the many ways they have utilized its power and speed to improve their own life. Finally, you'll learn about the long and heroic military history of the horse, stretching back more than 4,000 years.

Origin of Species

The remains of the animal that is—at least as of 2013—the oldest known ancestor of the horse were first discovered and identified in the nineteenth century. Originally, the animal was called Hyracotherium. It is now known as Eohippus, which is Greek for dawn horse. Eohippus was between 10 and 17 inches high at the shoulders, about 2 feet in length, and weighed approximately 12 pounds.

Through the ages Eohippus grew and evolved into what we know as the modern horse. Today, horses stand about 5 feet high or higher, are about 7 to 8 feet in length, and weigh about 1,000 pounds.

Riding Vocab

Hyracotherium is the name assigned to the Eohippus by the scientific community, but it's a mistake. The original discoverer of the species was Richard Owen, a nineteenth-century British paleontologist who is more famous for his work with dinosaurs (he was the one who coined the name dinosauria). He discovered the remains of the Eohippus in 1841 in England. He believed the creature was a member of the hyrax family, the ancestors of rabbits, among other species. So he named his discovery Hyracotherium, meaning "hyrax-like."

In 1876, Othniel Marsh unearthed more complete remains of the species in North America. He made the correct assessment that the specimen was an ancestor of the horse. He gave it the appropriate name of dawn horse, but, by the rules of paleontology, the earlier name given by Owen took priority. Even though it is in error, Hyracotherium continues as the scientific term for the Eohippus.

Not only was Eohippus a much smaller creature than the horse we know, but it also did not graze. It lived in North America, Asia, and Europe, lands that were covered by forests during that era.

Its diet and teeth were adapted to its environment. Eohippus was an herbivore, munching on leaves, plants, and fruits. The teeth of the species were not yet as sharp as they would become in the future, when its diet and environment would change.

Horse Sense

Through evolution, the horse's body changed to deal with the different climates of the earth. During the time and location of Eohippus, the earth resembled a modern rain forest. Conditions were damp and vegetation was deep. The multiple toes on the feet of Eohippus were useful to allow for easier walking over the soft grounds.

As the planet evolved over millions of years, the climate became drier. There was less forest on the earth and more open areas where grass grew.

With the horse no longer living in very damp conditions, the need for firmer footing declined. The feet of the species evolved to allow for easier movement and more speed. First, the horse's four-toed feet went to three toes, then to a central toe, and eventually to no toes—just a hoof.

Eohippus walked differently, too. The modern horse's flexible foot was many evolutionary steps into the future. Eohippus didn't have a hoof; it had a flat foot. It had four toes on its front feet and three on its hind feet, which also had a thick pad.

Mesohippus

Following Eohippus in the evolutionary chain of the horse were Orohippus, about 50 million years ago, and Epihippus, about 40 million years back. The next discernible ancestor of the horse is known as Mesohippus, which means "middle horse." Mesohippus dates back to about 35 million years ago.

In the 20 million years from Eohippus to Mesohippus, both the body and diet of the horse had to change. Living in more open spaces, Mesohippus needed to be able to travel further and faster than Eohippus, both to find food and to avoid enemies. Mesohippus's feet adapted to increase its ability to move. Mesohippus had just three toes on all feet.

Mesohippus developed stronger teeth than its predecessors. No longer did it have the nibbler's diet of leaves and plants. It needed to pull grass out of the ground. Mesohippus had six front teeth designed for grinding, which is similar to the teeth of the modern horse.

The legs of Mesohippus were longer and leaner than its predecessors. Its neck was also longer and more upright. Its back was straighter and did not have a bit of a hump in it, as was found on Eohippus.

With these changes, Mesohippus looked a lot more like the modern horse than Eohippus did, though it was still only about 2 feet, or 6 hands, high at the withers.

Riding Vocab

The height of a horse is measured in hands. Each hand is 4 inches, the approximate length across the palm. The horse is measured at the spot where the shoulder meets the neck, known as the withers. So if a horse is 64 inches high at the withers, he would be 16 hands. The inches between hands are shown in decimals, so a horse that is 65 inches is 16.1 hands.

An average riding horse is 15–16 hands; a pony is 14.2 hands or less. The great and quite powerful Thoroughbred Secretariat, subject of a popular 2010 movie, was 16.2 hands. Some draft horses such as the shire and the Brabant are much taller, occasionally reaching over 20 hands.

Miohippus and Merychippus

Mesohippus became extinct about 25 million years ago, but the species had already started to evolve into the larger Miohippus, which then evolved into Merychippus about 17 million years ago.

Merychippus was bigger than its predecessors, standing at about 40 inches at the shoulders, or 10 hands. Merychippus lived in herds that roamed the wide plains of North America. It developed stronger teeth to handle the thicker grasses of its North American domain.

The legs of Merychippus were longer, which gave it better movement to cover the large expanses. Also helping it run faster were its more powerful hindquarters and longer neck. The feet of Merychippus had also evolved. It still had three toes, but the center toe was the most prominent and took most of the weight.

Horse Sense

As the horse evolved, its brain grew larger. In particular, the brain of Merychippus was larger than that of its predecessors, presumably giving it greater intelligence.

The horse has always received criticism that it is not as smart as other animals, responding only with instinct and not with reason or cognition. But others dispute this. They will point out that a horse is usually quick to learn commands and is quite aware of his environment and handlers.

Dinohippus and Equus

About 12 million years ago, Merychippus evolved into Dinohippus. This version of the horse provided further refinements of the body and teeth. Then, about 4 million years ago, Equus evolved.

All of the traits of the modern horse were evident in Equus, including the sharp teeth for grazing, the long spine, and the powerful neck. It had just one hoof, not toes, on each foot. The long bone from the knee to the ankle, known as the cannon bone, the equivalent of the human shin, became longer and stronger. Equus was bigger than its predecessors, approximately 13.2 hands.

Equus was based in North America but spread over the land bridges of the time, eventually reaching into almost all parts of the world. Other species evolved during this expansion, including the zebra and the donkey.

Equus Descendants

From Equus there developed four distinct groups of horses, though it's not clear how they evolved into the modern breeds. The four groups are as follows:

1. Forest horse

2. Tarpan

3. Tundra horse

4. Asiatic wild horse (the only group that survives today)

The forest horse lived in Northern Europe. It was a thick, heavy horse, standing 15 hands high. It is probably the predecessor of the modern coldbloods such as the shire and Clydesdale, horses bred for their strength and size, not for riding or speed.

The tundra horse was so named because it roamed the frozen regions of Siberia and neighboring areas. There are no known descendants of the tundra horse. Also no longer surviving is the tarpan, which lived in the hills of Eastern Europe and died out during the nineteenth century.

The Asiatic wild horse is the only survivor of the four direct descendants of Equus. These horses are also known as Przewalski horses, named after the nineteenth-century Russian soldier who discovered and analyzed them. Originally, they ranged through most of Asia, but the Przewalski are now limited to the hills of Mongolia.

Domestication

The earliest drawings of horses that archaeologists have discovered are paintings in caves from approximately 17,000 years ago. The paintings indicate that the horse was still wild and the target of hunters.

It is now believed that the horse was originally domesticated as a source of food. A large number of horse bones have been discovered in caves in France, indicating that horses were killed for their meat.

Horse Sense

The number of horses in the world was declining rapidly just before the species was domesticated. Apparently, this was caused by the moderated temperatures that prevailed throughout the planet following the end of the last Ice Age about 11,000 years ago. The warmer conditions led to the widespread development of thick forest lands, which took away the grazing areas where the horse roamed. It's quite possible that the equine species might have become extinct if it had not been domesticated as a source for food.

The First Riders

By about 6,000 BC, horses were already being ridden. Archaeologists have found evidence of horses wearing bits from that period. They have found wear in the teeth of the remains of horses discovered in eastern Asia and dated to that time. There is also evidence of primitive horse equipment, such as a bridle made from animal bone.

The Horse at Work

It's not clear whether horses were ridden before they were used as draft animals. Though horses then (and now) were not as strong as oxen, they were definitely faster, which made horses more appealing for pulling carts and other equipment.

As the centuries passed, bigger breeds of horses with greater strength were developed for work in various capacities. They carried equipment, they helped till the land, and they transported people. They were not only quicker than oxen, but also able to move more easily on various types of ground. Their footing was much better on soft farm lands, where oxen could get bogged down.

Horses and ponies were used for various other jobs. They were used to transport coal in mines both above and below ground. Before the invention of engine-driven cars, they were used with rail lines. Standing to the side of the rails and attached to cars, they pulled the cargo forward to its destination. They did the same along canals, pulling vessels forward as they walked along the side of the water.

The Pony Express

The horse was not only good for business, but for government and civil work as well. Fire fighters and police officers needed horses in order to perform their jobs. The horse's mobility and long-distance traveling capability led to the creation of the Pony Express in the American west in 1860.

The rail lines of that period took a long time to deliver mail from the Midwest to California, sometimes more than a month. The Pony Express—which didn't use ponies, but rather a variety of fast breeds—could make the journey in two days.

The Pony Express was a very large, elaborate enterprise, with more than four hundred horses and well over one hundred riders. The horses were changed every 10 miles; the riders were changed every 100 miles.

The journeys of the Pony Express were fraught with danger from robbers, Native Americans who did not like the horses passing through their lands, and wild and dangerous animals.

Unfortunately, the large scope of the enterprise was very expensive and the Pony Express went out of business within a couple of years. Advances in roads and rails were soon able to take the place of the service. But even though it was short-lived, the legend of the Pony Express lives on.

Becoming Obsolete

In the nineteenth century, the development of steam engines eliminated the need for horses to pull rail cars and canal boats. In the twentieth century, stronger and more efficient devices began to replace most other uses of the horse. In mines, conveyor belts were developed, which were easy to operate and could carry heavier loads than horses or ponies could carry. And the development of the automobile and the airplane replaced the horse for most transportation needs.

Today, there are still horses in law enforcement and government, but they are mostly ceremonial. There are still places where the horse works, particularly in agriculture and ranching, but for the most part, the era of the working horse has passed.

The Horse in War

By 2000 BC, all the great powers of the era from Asia to the Middle East utilized the horse in warfare. The Hittites, Babylonians, Assyrians, Chinese, Greeks, and Egyptians all used horse-drawn chariots in combat. The Persian Empire, which came to dominate the region in the sixth century BC, developed its army of horses, its cavalry, to levels of efficiency never seen before.

As the centuries passed, mounted soldiers became more prominent in war. In the third century BC, the Parthian Empire achieved great success with its archers on horseback. They would ride ahead of their enemies, then wheel and shoot a lethal arrow at their pursuers.

As time went on and the horse became an increasing part of warfare, most empires tried to breed higher-quality horses. The Persians, Huns, and Chinese in particular used selective breeding to develop horses for war that were faster, stronger, and displayed more courage and intelligence.

The Muslim Empire had spread its grip of power from Arabia to Europe and North Africa during the first through the eighth centuries in great part because of the faster horses they had developed. Their mounts were known as the Arabian, a breed of horse that still flourishes today.

The Knights

King Charlemagne had great success with his mounted army during the eight century, driving out the invading Muslim forces. Following these triumphs, a new code of chivalry and honor was developed in Europe for professional soldiers on horseback called the Knights of Nobility. Eventually, they joined various Christian orders. Their high standards were listed as honor, valor, generosity, compassion, and loyalty.

In 1095, the Knights heeded the call of Pope Urban II for a Crusade. They headed to Jerusalem and the Holy Land to conquer the Arab forces and reclaim the land for Christianity.

Famous Horses in War

The most celebrated horse in antiquity was Bucephalus, the chosen mount of Alexander the Great. The Greek emperor rode Bucephalus into battle during all of his great conquests until the horse died of wounds suffered in the Battle of the Hydaspes in 326 BC. Alexander thought so much of his horse that he gave him a state funeral and named a city after him.

Twenty-one centuries later, another famous emperor, Napoleon, also had a favored mount. He was named Marengo, a white stallion Napoleon rode in many successful campaigns.

Napoleon had captured Marengo from the Turks after a battle in 1799. In turn, the British took him away from Napoleon after defeating the emperor in the Battle of Waterloo. The horse was then taken to Britain, where he was put on display. Marengo died at the advanced age of thirty-eight.

The Duke of Wellington conquered Napoleon at Waterloo. His mount during that battle was named Copenhagen. He was a well-bred Thoroughbred who had been a competitive race horse earlier in his life. After his success at Waterloo, Copenhagen returned to England hailed a hero. Like Alexander's Bucephalus more than 2,000 years before, Copenhagen received a state funeral when he died.

There were many other famous horses associated with the great military leaders. During the Roman Empire, the Emperor Caligula rode Incitatus, which when translated from the Latin means "swift." There was also Babieca, the mount of El Cid, the great Spanish general of the eleventh century.

Another of the most famous military horses of history was Traveller, the gray gelding who was the mount of Robert E. Lee during the Civil War. When Lee died, Traveller was part of the funeral procession. After Traveller died, he was buried in the graveyard at Washington and Lee University, though his body was later exhumed and displayed in exhibition. Eventually, Traveller's bones deteriorated. They were reburied at the University in 1971, a full century after the horse had died.

Modern Warfare

The horse continued to be a major part of warfare well into the twentieth century. Hundreds of thousands of horses were used in World War I, unfortunately with the same high levels of carnage that were encountered by the soldiers.

Horses were still evident in later conflicts, but usually only used as a last resort. When the Nazis tried to pull out of France near the end of World War II, all they had left were horse-drawn carriages. They were no match for the bombers employed by the Allied Forces.

The new technology of modern weapons and airplanes ended an era. After more than forty centuries, the horse was no longer a major part of warfare.

CHAPTER 2

Anatomy, Colors, and Vocalizations

In This Chapter

➤ The body of the horse

➤ Food and digestion

➤ Breeding, birth, and development

In this chapter, you'll learn about the modern horse. You'll learn how its body works and functions. You'll learn about the many colors and markings of the horse. You'll also learn about the way the horse eats and how it absorbs its food. Finally, you'll learn about the way the horse species continues, with information about breeding, pregnancy, birth, and early development.

The Horse's Head

The area at the top of a horse's head between and just behind his ears is called the poll. It is one of the hardest areas on a horse's body. It is the highest spot on a horse when he is standing erect.

There is an area of hair that hangs down between a horse's ears called the forelock. When a horse is wearing a bridle or a halter, you should make sure the forelock is straight rather than being pinched or turned in the wrong direction.

On a horse's face below his ears is the forehead, then the eyes, and on down to the long muzzle and the chin. On the underside of the muzzle is the jaw, with a long throat leading back to the horse's neck.

The Ears

The cartilage around a horse's ears is delicate, so anytime you're handling ears or the areas around them, you need to be careful. The ears are pointy and move about a great deal when the horse is trying to hear. As the horse tries to listen for sounds that might endanger his safety, his ears can turn close to 180 degrees.

The large and mobile ears of a horse allow for superior hearing as compared to humans. Horses can detect less audible sounds, and they can also hear sounds from further distances than humans can. Their superior hearing can also cause them to get easily upset by excessive noise. Loud sounds can unnerve these animals, which are usually quite on edge and worried about approaching enemies anyway.

The way a horse is carrying his ears is a good indication of his mood. An angry horse will pin his ears back, as will an aggressive or quite determined horse. But when a horse is not focused, his ears won't be as rigid. If a horse allows his ears to point down, he is usually very tired or unhappy—so unhappy that he has, at least temporarily, lost interest in everything.

Another bad sign is given when a horse has his ears turned back as far as possible toward where the rider is or would be sitting. This is usually an indication that the horse has been abused and is fearful of what the rider is going to do to him next.

A mare will turn back her ears when she is in heat and she senses that a stallion is coming up behind her.

The Eyes

The eyes of a horse are large, not only bigger than those of humans, but even bigger than the eyes of a whale. They are set wide apart, which gives the horse a larger viewing area to detect enemies.

A horse's field of vision is close to 360 degrees. Horses cannot see either directly behind or directly in front of themselves. That's why they are uncomfortable when someone walks straight at them. They can sense the presence of a person, but since their eyes are set so wide apart, they can't see them clearly.

A horse can see very well in dim light, better than humans can. This is another self-preserving trait the horse has developed in its many millions of years of evolution. The size and scope of a horse's eyes also let him see more clearly than his human handlers at longer distances.

Equine Tip

The vision of the horse can be a problem when there are quick changes in light. Shadows or sudden bright lights could possibly cause a horse to get frightened, or to spook. This can explain some otherwise unexplained problems you might have loading your horse onto a trailer, or doing virtually any other activity. It's a good idea to plan certain activities for times of the day when bright lights or shadows will not be an issue.

Horses do not have the type of depth perception that humans have, which is why they need to see a jump clearly before they leap. They need to be close to whatever they're jumping before they can figure out the right level of impulsion. That's why in competitions involving jumps or hurdles, the obstacle is always painted a different color from the surroundings. You will not, or should not, see a green jump set up in a field or course of grass.

The Nose

Also set wide apart are the nostrils, which are wide and deep. The long snout of the horse provides extra space for the nasal passages to function. The long nostrils are the main reason that most horse breeds aren't bothered by cold temperatures. The long passages warm the air before the horse inhales it.

The nose also provides the horse with a strong sense of smell. As with the horse's hearing and vision, a horse's sense of smell is more acute than a human's. It is one more way that the jittery horse, known as a flight animal, can detect approaching enemies and threats.

Horse Sense

Horses are considered flight animals, which means they are easily frightened and are ready to take off at any indication of an approaching predator.

Even though most horses now are domesticated and under no real threat of attack, their urge to flee has not left them. That is why they need to be handled and approached in certain ways to prevent them from getting scared or becoming enraged.

A horse's sense of smell is also more acute than a human's; horses can detect scents from much longer distances than can humans. Scents can alert horses when dangerous predators have entered their area. Thirsty and hungry horses in the wild can also detect the distant scent of ponds and streams, as well as the aromas of food sources.

The horse's sense of smell is also used to recognize other horses. A mare and her foal will quickly learn each other's scents. A stallion will also use his strong sense of smell to detect the scent of a mare in heat.

A horse can inhale air only through his nose. That's why you never see a horse panting like a dog.

The Teeth

The horse's teeth are one of its most distinctive and complicated features. Horses are born with no teeth, though they begin to appear within two weeks. The baby teeth, used for nursing, are called milk teeth. They are fully in place after nine months until about age two. The adult teeth then begin to appear. They continue to grow about ⅛ inch every year.

Adult male horses have twenty teeth; females have eighteen. The different totals are because the males develop two canine teeth by the age of five, whereas the female does not. A horse has twelve molars and six incisors. The teeth have long crowns, as long as 3½ inches, with short roots.

Special features come and go in the horse's teeth, which is why an expert can tell a horse's age just by looking at his teeth. Hooks and grooves appear on different teeth and later disappear. The angle of the horse's teeth changes as the horse grows older. The surface of the teeth also shows wear with time.

A horse's mouth has an open area to the side called the bar. This is the spot where the bit of the bridle is connected to the mouthpiece.

The Horse's Body

There are many physical variations among the breeds of horses, with differences in shoulder slopes, neck arches, and leg lengths. But for most horses, a rule of thumb for conformation is that their height from the ground to the withers should be the same as the length from the withers to the tail.

Ideally, from the neck back, the horse should be divided equally in three parts:

1. The shoulders

2. The back

3. The hindquarters

The horse's muscles are quite flexible and elastic while also being quite powerful. The strength of the muscles is dependent on the strength of the tendons, which hold them together and attach them to the bones.

Many of the names of the horse's muscles are familiar from the human body, such as deltoids, quadriceps, and biceps. Horses also have muscles located near the top of the tail.

The Neck

There are seven bones in a horse's neck, which through many millions of years of evolution grew to be very strong and powerful. The neck of a stallion is particularly notable for its scope and power.

A horse's long neck is particularly useful when it comes to jumping. It provides the power that allows leverage for the rest of the body to extend.

The area along the top of the neck is known as the crest. This is where the mane of the horse grows. The neck then goes into the back, which goes into the loins and the hindquarters.

The withers should flow naturally from the neck and forward from the back. If the withers are too elevated or too low, it will be difficult to fit a saddle on the horse, among other problems.

The Shoulder and Back

The scapula bone lies in front of the rib cage and then connects to the shoulder, which then bends around the ribs to join up with the elbow joint. In the other direction, the elbow then connects to the leg. For most breeds, the shoulder should be long and sloping. This allows the horse to have easier movement.

On the top of the horse, the vertebrae of the spine run down the back toward the tail. The lumbar sacral joint connects to the hip and then goes down to the hind legs.

The Front Legs

The top part of the front legs is known as the forearm, which connects through the knee to the hard cannon bone. The fetlock is the equine equivalent of the human ankle. It connects to the pastern, the flexible part of the foot that goes down to the hoof. The outside of the hoof is called the coronet.

There are other features on the horse's legs that are apparently leftover items from evolution and no longer have any use. Above the knee on each leg of the horse is a small growth known as a chestnut. Sometimes the skin of the chestnut is removed, though this may give pain to the horse. More often, it is just trimmed, which usually doesn't bother the horse.

A similar object on the legs of some horses is called an ergot, which is located down by the fetlock. Like the chestnut, an ergot is usually covered with hair and not so easy to see.

The Back Legs

The area at the top of the back legs is called the stifle. If a horse injures this part of the leg and pulls this muscle, it's called grabbing a stifle. While the front legs are straight—or at least should be—the back legs are angled back from the hips to the back knee, which is called the hock. The part of the leg from the hip down to the back knee is called the gaskin.

The rest of the terms for the back legs are the same as the front legs with the addition of the word hind (hind cannon, hind fetlock, etc.)

The back legs should be angled forward from the hock to the fetlock. But being angled too far forward is an undesirable trait called a sickle hock.

If the hocks are too close together, offering the appearance of knock-knees, this is another conformation fault called cow hocks.

Both of these traits will put too much pressure on a horse's legs. If you're selecting a horse to own, you should avoid horses with either of these problems.

The Feet

The feet of a horse are extremely important and a place of many potential problems. The horse's foot has two parts. The bottom half of the foot containing the hoof has no nerve endings, which is why a shoe can be nailed into it.

The horse's front feet are slightly curved, or concave; the back foot slightly more. The back part of the hoof is called the frog, which acts like a shock absorber. The bar of the foot is further up on the back of the hoof. The remaining front part of the foot is known as the wall.

Equine Tip

A wide foot is considered good for moving over hills and heavily grassed areas. A small foot is considered helpful for moving on soft or damp footing. A horse with a wide foot is more prone to sliding in wet conditions and may have trouble keeping his balance.

The hoof of the foot grows approximately ¼ to 3/8 inch every month. This is the main reason a horse needs to have his shoes changed about every month or so. After a farrier removes the old shoe, he trims down the excess growth of the hoof before he puts on a new shoe. This is known as rasping.

Hot Shoeing

After a foot has been prepared for a shoe, the farrier often puts a hot shoe onto the spot where the actual shoe will go. This marks a location for the shoe and clears off the area on the hoof in preparation. The hot shoe is also designed to sterilize the foot, as the heat will burn off all bacteria and fungi from the area.

The shoe goes around the rim of the hoof wall, and is nailed in place. Usually, this takes four nails on the outside and three on the inside. The nails have to be placed in the correct spot, which is the outside part of the wall of the hoof, or the horse may become sore or lame.

Horse Colors

There are a handful of basic colors on a horse and then there are a number of variations within those colors. Depending on the breed, certain colors may be known by one name on one breed but a different name on another. For example, some breeds, including Standardbreds, include brown as one of the colors, but the same shade is always called "dark bay or brown" on Thoroughbreds.

The basic colors are black, brown, red, and yellow. There are some pure white horses, called albinos, but they are quite rare.

Dark Colors

Pure black horses are not that common in any breed; shades of brown are much more common. Horses can be listed as brown, but in many breeds the color is called dark bay. Bay is a bit lighter than brown, and it is the most common of the brown colors.

Shades of Red

Most horse breeds with light red coats are called chestnut. Sorrel is the darker version of chestnut, and blond is a lighter shade. Not all breeds use sorrel or blond to differentiate the shades of chestnut.

Light Shades

A gray horse is a mixture of black and white colors. A roan is a mixture of white and chestnut, sometimes known as a strawberry roan. Both grays and roans tend to lose their dark hairs as they get older. At an advanced age, they are usually all white, which can sometimes be stunning to someone who knew how the horse looked when it was younger.

Yellows

Dun is a yellow or gold coat, though it can also contain many other shades. A similar color is palomino, another shade of yellow, most prominently worn by the palomino breed.

Combinations

Grays and roans are examples of combinations, but there are others as well. Buckskin is a combination of a dark color with some yellow. Other breeds, such as the pinto and the Appaloosa, have multicolored coats with various patterns and spotting on their bodies.

Face Markings

When a horse is wearing a bridle or blinders, you may not notice the color pattern on his face. But there are a number of distinctive markings on the faces of horses. Most of the markings are white surrounded by dark colors.

➤ Strip: a narrow patch of white hair that runs down the middle of the face

➤ Blaze: an even larger strip down the middle

➤ Bald: a design of white hair that covers an even wider area than a strip or blaze

➤ Star: a marking around the eyes

➤ Snip: a small mark around the nose

Horse Vocalizations

The ways in which the horse communicates can be broken down into four categories:

1. Nasal sounds

2. Nickers

3. Loud vocalizations

4. Whinnies

Nasal Sounds

A snort is a sound a horse makes through the vibrations of his nasal passages. It is a way that horses signal each other about possible threats that they have detected. It is not a very loud sound because it's designed to alert other horses to a distant threat without being heard by the animal being perceived as the threat. The sound of the snort takes close to a full second.

Similar to a snort is a blow. This sound is also created through the nose, but it is a gentler and friendlier sound or greeting.

Nickers

Nickers are low sounds that come through a horse's throat. The basic nicker sound is given as a greeting, either to another horse or a friendly handler. It is not a very loud sound and can't be heard over a long distance.

Mares use nickers when communicating with their young foals. It is a distinctive sound that the foal recognizes and responds to quickly.

A nicker can also be heard from stallions as a way of communicating with a mare before a mating session.

Loud Vocalizations

Horses utilize much louder sounds when they are either agitated or really excited. These include a squeal, a loud sound made by a horse that feels threatened. A squeal is given as a strong warning that the horse is ready to take further action to deal with what he feel is a threat.

Even louder than squeals are roars and screams. These loudest equine sounds are usually heard only in the wild among horses that have found some reason to become extremely angry.

The Whinny

A sound that starts out like a loud squeal but ends as a more peaceful nicker is called a neigh, or a whinny. It is the loudest of the sounds made by horses and it can be heard over the longest distances.

A whinny is a way for horses to communicate with each other when they have become separated. Mares and their foals in particular will communicate in this manner. Normally, when one whinny is given, the other horse for whom it was intended will respond with a similar whinny.

CHAPTER 3

Horse Breeds

In This Chapter

➤ Riding and jumping horses

➤ Colorful coats

➤ Mixed and unknown bloodlines

➤ The big horses

In this chapter, you'll learn all about the most popular horse breeds in the world. You'll learn about the horses bred for their speed and jumping ability. You'll learn about the horses most known for their fancy colors. You'll also learn about the horses bred for their size and power.

Hotbloods, Warmbloods, Coldbloods

Horses come in so many different sizes and have so many different uses that people came up with a way to categorize each breed. The three main categories are as follows:

1. Hotblood: Horses bred for speed, including the Arabian and its descendant, the Thoroughbred. These horses are noted not only for their powerful legs and quickness, but for their temperamental and high-strung nature as well.

2. Warmblood: Horses that may look and perform like hotbloods but are usually not as difficult to handle. They can also be quite athletic and agile and are the most successful horses in the show rings because of their jumping ability and even temperament.

3. Coldblood: Large, powerful horses, often twice as big as the average hotblood or warmblood. They were developed as work and combat horses, both for their size and their great hauling capabilities. The coldbloods are also the friendliest of the horse breeds, usually easy to get along with and quite cooperative.

Runners and Jumpers

Every domesticated horse breed was developed for a purpose, either for transportation or for specific work such as herding. For many of the smaller and more athletic breeds, these original purposes have disappeared, but the horses have been adapted for the show rings and other sporting uses.

Andalusian

The Andalusian is one of the most notable of the many Spanish breeds that still flourish in modern times. They are a sturdy, with strong legs, knees, and feet.

Though Andalusians, like Thoroughbreds, are descended from Arabians, they do not have the speed of that breed. Since they also don't have the Thoroughbred's powerful neck and shoulders, they also lack the Thoroughbred's imposing physical presence. However, the Andalusian is an athletic horse that is noted for its good movement. Its gait is particularly smooth and elegant.

The official registries of the Andalusian now list nearly 200,000 members of the breed worldwide. The majority of modern-day Andalusians, especially those bred in the United States, are gray. They are also noted for having a particularly thick mane and tail.

The Andalusian is a visually attractive breed. Though its neck lacks the scope of other hotbloods, it is quite muscular and powerful in appearance, especially when the horse is moving in a collected tro, a stride which draws, or "collects," the horse's strength into its neck and back.

Andalusians have been established for more than five hundred years. In earlier times, they were seen often on the battlefield. Today, they are seen competing in a number of sporting activities, both English and western. With their soundness, athleticism, and natural aggressiveness, they are excellent jumpers.

Arabian

The Arabian is the oldest known breed of riding horse in the world and the ancestor of many other breeds that exist today. Used by the Bedouin tribes through much of Europe and Western Africa 1,000 to 2,000 years ago, the Arabian was then faster than any other horse being ridden. Though some of its descendants, including the Thoroughbred, are now bigger and faster, the Arabian is still one of the quickest breeds and is particularly noted for its stamina.

The modern Arabian is another breed that can be found in a wide variety of riding activities, both English and western. The breed also is featured in horse shows restricted to Arabians.

Arabians are among the most valuable breeds in the world today because of their appearances in show rings and their speed on race tracks.

Criollo

The Criollo is one of the Spanish breeds brought to North America in the sixteenth century by conquering conquistadores. It is a descendant of the Andalusian, but was developed in the wild among feral horses. Several centuries after arriving from Europe, Criollos were captured from the wild and eventually bred to other breeds more noted for their sturdiness.

The modern criollo bloodlines were created more than a century ago. It is now a very popular breed in South America, especially in Uruguay, but also in Argentina, Chile, and Peru.

The Criollo, which roughly translates from the Spanish to mean locally raised, is not as big as most riding horses. The average member of the breed is just barely above the height of a pony, usually below 15 hands. But Criollos are very good movers and are often seen in the show rings of South America.

The Criollo is particularly noted for its stamina. There are many competitive long-distance races for the breed. The strength and good movements of the Criollo make the breed excellent Argentine polo ponies, which are considered to be the best in the world.

Dutch Warmblood

One of the most successful horses in the formal competitions of dressage and show jumping, the Dutch warmblood is quite athletic, particularly known for its jumping ability. Standing a little over 15 hands high, it is about average size for a warmblood, not as big as a Thoroughbred but bigger than a Criollo. It is known in particular for its soundness and longevity.

The Dutch warmblood is now at the top of the list of all breeds when it comes to producing outstanding horses for the show ring. These days, there are more Dutch warmbloods than any other breed that are dressage champions.

Hanoverian

Originally, Hanoverians were used for their efficiency at pulling carriages, but they were also adapted for work on farms. In the twentieth century, their use for riding increased, and it has continued to expand as the Hanoverian has shown its prowess in competition.

Hanoverians are very successful in all forms of English-riding sports, including all jumping and dressage events. Their success has made the breed one of the most expensive in the world, with the best prospects selling at auction for hundreds of thousands of dollars.

Icelandic

Iceland is better known for the ponies it produces, but the Icelandic horse has a history that can be traced back more than a thousand years. It is the only full-sized horse on this isolated island, and it is noted for its soundness and good movements.

All the modern descendants possess the heartiness of the breed, which had been developed over hundreds of generations. The harsh conditions of its home island are considered one of the primary reasons for the Icelandic horse to be so sturdy and dependable. Through the many centuries of bad weather and frequent volcanic eruptions, only the finest specimens of the breed could survive in Iceland.

One of the most unusual attributes of the Icelandic is its hair. To deal with the wintry conditions, the modern Icelandic horse has the distinctive feature of a double coat.

The Icelandic is considered a horse, although in size it is actually a pony. It is less than 14 hands high and weighs less than 900 pounds. The breed is not particularly rangy, nor is its appearance that impressive. No one would ever describe an Icelandic horse as looking sleek. By equine standards, its neck is unusually short and quite sturdy like the rest of it.

Horse Sense

Unlike most breeds, the Icelandic horse isn't a flight animal. This is because there are no natural enemies, other than humans, of the horse in Iceland. There are breeders who raise the Icelandic strictly for its meat.

The Icelandic is trained to move in a distinctive gait, the tölt, which is a fancy lateral amble. Only certain members of the breed who possess the proper agility and leg movement are trained to move in the tölt. The rest are used for other purposes, including draft work.

The Icelandic is one of the healthiest and fertile horses in the world. A main reason for this is that the Icelandic government has strict laws governing the importation of horses. They have even set high standards for the gear that can be used on the breed.

The distinctive Icelandic horse is popular throughout the world. There are Icelandic riding clubs in much of Europe as well as in South America. There are also many enthusiastic breeders and importers of Icelandic horses in the United States, including some stables that have them available for riding.

Morgan

The Morgan is a distinctly American breed, tracing back to near the end of the eighteenth century. The foundation sire of the breed, named Justin Morgan after its owner, may have been a Thoroughbred, though his exact breeding is unknown. But through a small group of his sons, the Morgan breed developed, first in New England and then throughout the country. Morgans are prominent in the development of other breeds as well, including the quarter horse, the Tennessee walking horse and the Missouri fox trotter.

The Morgan became popular because it was well made, with good movement. It was also quite versatile. The Morgan was used in many of the more common equine activities in the pre-automobile era. It was a popular mount of the period and was also used frequently to pull carriages. There were also many races, particularly cart races, that featured Morgans.

Through the nineteenth century, the Morgan was noted as the most prominent horse breed used by American cavalry officers. It was the mount of choice for both sides during the Civil War.

The Morgan remains popular today because it is an attractive horse and easier to ride than most warmbloods. It is strong without being overwhelming and has a friendly temperament. Morgans can be seen in all types of horse competitions, both English and western. Many Morgans are also found at stables and other locations where you can learn to ride.

Oldenburg

The Oldenburg is an athletic horse with excellent jumping ability. The breed was developed in the eighteenth century in the German land of Oldenburg. Originally, it was a cross of the large local mares with stallions imported from Turkey and Spain.

The Oldenburg is a big and rangy horse, usually over 16 hands high. It is a very popular breed in North America. Dozens if not hundreds of riding academies offer lessons and rides with Oldenburgs. Their gaits are extremely fluid, rhythmical, and proper. These attributes make them highly successful in the dressage show rings and very valuable at auction.

Peruvian Paso

The Peruvian paso is one of the best moving horses in the world. It is known for its fancy and rapid ambling gait, which it can perform on the roads and trails of South America at speeds above 30 miles per hour.

The Peruvian paso is not a particularly big horse, usually standing about 15 hands high and weighing about 1,000 pounds. It is one of the many descendants of the horses brought from Spain to North and South America in the sixteenth century by the conquistadores.

Its special gaits were developed in South America by the owners of large plantations. They needed a horse that was smooth to ride while covering a lot of ground quickly. The four-beat gait that the Peruvian Paso developed not only let it move fast but minimized the jars and bounces for the rider. That's why the breed is considered one of the most comfortable horses to ride today.

In the Peruvian paso show competitions of South America, it is a standard practice for the judges themselves to ride the horses in order to determine which competitor offers the smoothest ride.

Quarter Horse

The modern quarter horse was originally developed in the American West to deal with the many tasks of the cowboys working on ranches with cattle and other animals. It's an agile and quick horse, known for its fast bursts of speed, which are very useful when moving through and around herds.

The quarter horse, more formally known as the American quarter horse, was developed from many of the breeds of wild horses that roamed the American West in the nineteenth century.

Virtually every activity of cowboys, from roping to cutting and penning, utilized the quarter horse. Today, the sports that were created from these activities and are now the featured events in rodeos still use the quarter horse above all other breeds.

Quarter horse racing is also popular, particularly in the Southwest and California. In Texas, Oklahoma, and New Mexico, quarter horse racing rivals Thoroughbred racing in popularity.

The name quarter horse comes from the breed's ability to run fast up to a quarter mile. The most important quarter horse races, which can each be worth many millions of dollars, are all at a quarter mile. Most of the other races in the sport, contested by cheaper horses, are run at shorter distances, from 300–400 yards.

With the breed involved in so many activities, it's not surprising that quarter horses are among the most plentiful horses in the world, with more than five million registered. They are also a very popular horse for pleasure riding, especially in the West. It should not be hard to find a quarter horse to ride or to buy.

Standardbred

The standardbred is primarily a race horse, bred to carry carts in competition. The breed developed in the nineteenth century, tracing to a foundation Thoroughbred sire, Hambletonian. Standardbreds include both pacers, which race with lateral gaits, and trotters, which use the diagonal gait.

Riding Vocab

The word standard is in the name of the standardbred because in the early days of the breed, the horse had to run up to a certain speed—the standard—in order to be registered and raced.

In North America, virtually all of the thousands of standardbred races are run at 1 mile, though in Europe, many races are run at longer distances. Standardbred racing, also known as harness racing, is popular in France and particularly popular in Sweden, perhaps the only location in the world where the sport is more popular than Thoroughbred races over the flat.

Riding Vocab

The "Flat" is a term for a course which horses race over when it doesn't include any hurdles. The horses in these races are sometimes called "runners," to differentiate them from Standardbreds who are either trotting or pacing.

After a standardbred's racing career is over, he is often introduced to saddles for the first time. It's fairly common to see a notice of a standardbred for sale at age ten or older with a note that the horse has just recently been saddled and is performing well. It is one way to make further use and prolong the life of these gallant animals. In the past, most standardbreds that were no longer capable of racing were just discarded and often sold to butchers, a practice that is now illegal in many states.

Tennessee Walking Horse

Originally a working horse, the Tennessee walking horse has now evolved into one of the most popular show horses in the world. Its distinctive amble, with its front legs curling up with every step, provides quite an entertaining show. There is a large industry that trains the breed for public appearances. These events have become increasingly popular during the last fifty years.

Originally, the horse was seen on southern farms. Landowners were trying to develop horses that could move around their large plantations quickly while providing a comfortable seat for the rider. The breed was established by combining various breeds, including Thoroughbreds and Morgans. Eventually, the stride of the horse became so distinctive that they were developed for outdoor entertainment.

Though they have a niche in the show ring all their own, Tennessee walking horses can be found competing in other events, minus their high steps. They have had success in most western riding sports, as well as in jumping and other English equestrian sports.

The breed is considered to be one of the easiest horses to ride. Many riders who have physical problems, such as back pain, find the Tennessee walking horse, with its easy-going manner and smooth step, to be their most comfortable mount. For those same reasons, the horse is also often used in programs that provide rides for the physically handicapped.

Because their stride is quite specialized, a number of riding academies offer lessons on how to ride the horse. They teach the proper way to distribute your weight and how to get your horse into the proper rhythm so that he can makes his fancy high steps.

Thoroughbred

The most valuable breed in the world, the Thoroughbred is the fastest breed of horse, and that's not by accident. It is bred for speed and for racing. Its powerful legs and body can generate long, extended strides while reaching speeds up to 45 miles per hour.

The Thoroughbred breed can be traced back to three oriental stallions that were brought to England (after being stolen or kidnapped) in the seventeenth and early eighteenth centuries. Its hot blood was then crossed with the stockier breeds that then existed in England. The new breed maintained the speed of its sires and the strength of its dams. The Thoroughbred developed long and lean legs with hard muscles and a long stride that made it faster than all other horses.

The original traits of the Thoroughbred still exist in the breed all these centuries later, along with a great deal of refinement. Originally, the breed raced over long distances of 10 miles or more. Now, much of that stamina has been replaced by more speed. Most thoroughbred races, especially in the United States, are under 1 mile.

Many other breeds have been developed with Thoroughbred bloodlines, including other racing animals such as the standardbred and the quarter horse. Many of the prominent breeds from the show rings also have a good deal of Thoroughbred in their history, including the Trakehner and the Dutch warmblood.

The Thoroughbred continues to flourish as a racing animal and is popular around the world. There are multibillion-dollar Thoroughbred racing industries on six different continents.

If you're just beginning, you might find a Thoroughbred docile enough to ride, but remember that many Thoroughbreds are excitable, on edge, and not always that cooperative. That is why they are known as hotbloods. They are more difficult to control than your average warmblood, not to mention your friendly coldblood.

Trakehner

The Trakehner is a horse from Eastern Europe noted for its leaping ability. Developed in the eighteenth century, Trakeners are about average height—16 hands—but they have a lighter build than most other warm-blooded horses. This gives them added maneuverability and makes them useful over a jumping course.

The Trakehner was named after the region in East Prussia where they were developed. In the nineteenth century, the local horses were bred to larger and stronger Thoroughbreds, which created the strong and agile modern Trakehner.

Colorful Horses

Certain breeds are best known by the color of their coat. They can have one unusual color or a combination of several. The look of their hair makes each one of these breeds very popular for riding and owning.

Appaloosa

A horse known for its distinctive coloring is the Appaloosa. Its coat is spotted, normally referred to as leopard spots. A dark base color is covered with white blotches. No two Appaloosa coats are exactly the same, though usually the spotting is near the hips and the horse's hindquarters.

There are plenty of ancient cave paintings and more recent etchings that depict horses with spotted coats. Many spotted horses were brought to the Americas by Spaniards in the sixteenth century. Eventually, many of the spotted horses were taken over and raised by the Nez Percé tribes of the West, who used selective breeding to develop the Appaloosa.

Riding Vocab

The Appaloosa got its name from the Nez Percé tribes. The Palouse River of Washington and Idaho was in Nez Percé territory. Appaloosa was derived from the river's name.

After many battles, the Nez Percé tribes were defeated late in the nineteenth century, and great numbers of their Appaloosa horses were eliminated, released, or captured. But the breed was revitalized in the twentieth century. The number of registered Appaloosas is now one of the highest of any breed in the world. The selective breeding of the Nez Percé created a tough and durable breed with a coat that makes it very popular.

Paint

One more horse that owes much of its popularity to its coat is the paint. It does not have a spotted coat like an Appaloosa, but it does have broad patterns of alternating dark and light colors.

There is no particular pattern to the colors of paints. They can have a white hip or a white shoulder or some other combination. The patterns can be mixed, spotted, or whatever other terms you might like to use, such as splashy or chromatic.

All paint horses are required to be direct descendants of Thoroughbred, quarter horse or paint parents. The breed is distinguished in this manner from the pinto, a separate breed with similar colors.

Like the quarter horse, the paint is considered a good-moving and sturdy horse that can be used in many capacities, including racing.

Palomino

The only noted breed that has a color named after it is the palomino. Its coat, which is a cream color with a hint of brown, gold, and tan, and its tail, which is a lighter version of the same color, are the most famous features of this quite popular breed.

The origin of the palomino is difficult to determine. Horses of this very distinctive color were described in ancient times. They were a favorite of royalty and a prized gift between kings. They were among the horses sent to the Americas by the Spanish during the sixteenth century. The breed then became closely associated with the West. That connection continues today, with the palomino being a popular horse in western sports as well as in parades and other public events.

There have been some famous palominos on television, though mostly on black-and-white film, which didn't particularly display their distinctive color. Roy Rogers' Trigger was a palomino, as was the horse that could talk, at least on television, Mr. Ed (who could also drive a truck, among other skills). Both Trigger and Mr. Ed were fully registered with the Palomino Horse Association.

Mixed Breeds

These horses are not one specific breed. They may be a mixture of two or more breeds, but they do not have their own registries.

Polo Ponies

Polo ponies are not ponies but horses, though in the earlier days of the sport, ponies were utilized. But now the sport requires horses, normally warmbloods or hotbloods.

In Europe and North America, polo ponies are often derived from Thoroughbred bloodlines. South America has been home of the best polo playing for many decades. The best polo ponies in South America—and probably in the world—are often descendants of the local Criollo horse.

Wherever they come from, polo ponies require a lot of training to be used during a match. They have to get used to the physical contact that is allowed in the sport as well as the quick and unusual movements of their riders.

Polo ponies are often active for a long time. Usually, they don't become active participants in the sport until they reach the age of five. Then they continue to compete well past the age of ten.

Usually, each player on a polo team owns and cares for his own ponies, though a number of teams may have a sponsor who takes care of the bills. But because the sport can offer lucrative returns to its top competitors, the polo pony is usually given lavish attention and treated with great care, which helps to explain its longevity.

Riding Vocab

Mustang is actually a Spanish word that means "vagabond" or "homeless."

Mustang

Perhaps the most famous wild horse of the West, the mustang is one more horse brought to America by Spaniards and then allowed to roam the open spaces east of the Pacific. Through the years, as other horses were set free in the West, they mixed in with the already wild horses. As a result, the current mustang has many different strains from other breeds. A debate actually rages among horse people as to whether the modern mustang is really a separate breed.

Since its earliest days in North America, the mustang has been captured and tamed to be used for riding or as a source of food. Until recent years there were many horsemen who specialized in breaking and training mustangs to be ridden.

With the decrease in their roaming land and the capture of so many mustangs during the nineteenth and twentieth centuries, the breed's numbers dropped dramatically. More than 2 million mustangs roamed the West in 1900. That number is now down to well under 100,000, maybe lower because the Bureau of Land Management has created a mustang adoption program.

Horse Sense

Wild horses are able to survive better than most other animals in the wild because of their ability to move. They can travel long distances at rapid clips in order to find the water and food that they need to survive. Wild cattle, among other animals, are unable to move quickly or cover enough ground to survive as well in dry lands.

Domestic Mustangs

Those who adopt or ride newly domesticated mustangs shouldn't expect them to be uncontrollable. Yes, they used to roam in the wild, but chances are they've come to appreciate the comforts of domestic life. They no longer have to search for food and water, nor seek shelter in bad weather. They can also learn to like and be devoted to people.

There might be the occasional flashback and otherwise inexplicable out-of-control moment, especially when you try to ride them, but most domesticated mustangs get through it and then grow to appreciate tender and loving care.

Grade Horses

Grade horses are the equine equivalent of mutts in the dog world. Many of them are of no specific breed, at least no known breed, with no papers. Other grade horses might be the result of a mixed mating between two breeds, quite possibly unplanned or resulting from a mix-up or mistake.

As a result of his breeding, or lack thereof, a grade horse is never going to have the value of a purebred. However, that doesn't mean grade horses aren't useful and possibly a wonderful riding horse and companion. There have been examples of grade horses that have achieved great success in various horse competitions. While there are many events that require a horse to have proper breeding, others have no such requirements.

If you're new to horses and looking to buy one to ride, you'll be able to get a good bargain on a grade horse. While there may be some horse people who will look down their nose at grade horses, there's no reason for you to be one of them.

Coldbloods

The biggest horses were developed for their strength and endurance. Most of them were developed in the cold climates of Europe and Eastern Asia. Many were developed in mountainous regions, where the uneven terrain made transportation difficult, especially the transportation of heavy loads.

Before the development of mechanical and engine-powered transportation, the strong horse offered the best way for farmers and others to get their products to market. The ox was too slow, and smaller horses could not haul as big a load.

By the twentieth century, as more efficient engines were developed and became accessible, the need for the big horses declined, as did their numbers.

Belgian Draft Horses

Noted particularly for their power and size, Belgian draft horses are capable of pulling tremendous loads. The breed, which is usually known in America simply as the Belgian, is becoming increasingly popular as a riding horse. It is much bigger than any warm-blooded or hot-blooded horse, normally standing over 18 hands high while weighing about 1 ton, though some members of the breed have weighed over 3,000 pounds. But their temperament is very kind and they are easy to handle.

The Belgian has powerful and steady legs, but with its great size, don't expect it to generate much speed or have any proficiency over jumps.

The Belgian comes in a variety of colors, though shades of red and gray are the most common.

Even though they are easy-going, the immense size of Belgians limits the amount of riders who can get on their back and control them.

Clydesdale

Made popular by a beer commercial, the Clydesdale is not quite as big as some of the other cold-blooded breeds, most notably the shire and the Belgian, but Clydesdales are still a lot bigger than most riding horses. They stand anywhere from 16 to 18 hands, and weigh close to 2,000 pounds.

Riding Vocab

The hair that grows around the knees and ankles on horses, particularly large ones, are called feathers. The large breeds are celebrated for the attractive design of their feathering.

The Clydesdale is one of the more recently established breeds, having been developed in Scotland in the nineteenth century. Naturally, with its size, it was bred for its power rather than its ride-ability. But there are many Clydesdales now ridden under saddle, though, as with other big horses, they lack the speed and leaping ability of the smaller equines.

Like many of the bigger breeds, the Clydesdales are known for the heavy hair that grows on their legs.

Friesian

The Friesian is the large draft horse of the Netherlands, though it is not as big as many coldbloods. It stands from 15 to 17 hands high and weighs somewhere around 1,500 pounds.

Equine Tip

It's not surprising that almost all of the cold-blooded breeds come from wintry, northern climates. That's why they're called coldbloods, since the blood flowing through their veins in as hot as that of any other equine.

The large draft horses are likely the descendants of the large forest horse developed before recorded time. They have been bred to carry large loads while not being noted for their speed. In wintry conditions, with narrow roads often blocked by snow, there was never much need for a fast-moving, quick-shifting horse, but plenty of use could be made of a powerful animal capable of carrying heavy loads through difficult fields and roads.

The Friesian breed can be traced back a long way, more than twenty centuries. It was the combat mount of the ancient Dutch knights as well as the draft horses used for local farming. It is one of the most maneuverable of the large breeds, probably owing to the crossing of the breed with smaller horses a few centuries ago.

The Friesian breed came close to extinction at the end of World War I, with its numbers reduced to just a handful. But the Friesian was saved by dedicated breeders and once again flourishes.

Because of its good movement and great strength, the Friesian is particularly successful in dressage competitions. It is also visually stunning, with a long, flowing mane and a dark black color. The Friesian is a calm, friendly type and is usually easy for a rider to handle. But, as with other large breeds, make sure you're big enough to handle one before you get aboard.

Percheron

The Percheron is a big, powerful horse, usually used to pull carts and other items. It has a kind and gentle nature, which makes it popular as a horse under saddle.

The Percheron was developed in France more than four hundred years ago. It was imported to America in large numbers in the nineteenth century. It soon became the main draft horse in the country. As the need for large horses began to disappear in the mid-twentieth century, the Percheron's numbers began to dwindle. But there are still many thousands of them in North America as well as throughout their home continent of Europe.

The Percheron is about 17 hands high or higher and weighs close to 1 ton. It has been a popular choice for farm work because of the lack of feathering on its legs. This meant that

Percherons would not pick up as much mud or other debris as the other large breeds, which are noted for their feathering.

The Percheron possesses great stamina as well as strength. In the nineteenth century, when its use was much more common, the Percheron was known to be able to travel as much as 40 miles in a day, a long distance for a horse pulling a heavy load.

Among horse fanciers, the Percheron's distinctive gray and black colors make it an easy breed to spot. It has now become quite popular in the show ring; its colors and large presence makes it a crowd favorite at horse events throughout the world.

Riding Vocab

In Britain, one of the first activities of large horses was to carry ale out of breweries to the pubs and other locations where it was sold. However, this is not the reason that horses were known as draft, or in England, draught horses. The derivation comes from an old English word, dragan, meaning to haul or carry.

Shire

The Shire is a British draft horse, one of the biggest and strongest of all horses. Originally, it was bred to support the medieval knights who went into battle carrying hundreds of pounds of gear. The shire later began what's now known as the work of the draft horse, pulling wagons with huge loads.

The shire is normally at least 17 hands tall, though some members of the breed have grown above 20 hands (which means the top of their head was about 8 feet off the ground.) It weighs at least 1 ton, though some shores have been much heavier.

As with most large breeds, the uses of the shire began to decline with the development of machines and engines that could do the same work more efficiently. The numbers of the breed began to decline rapidly in the twentieth century.

Although many of the shires are simply too big to ride, there are slightly smaller shires that are trained to be ridden under saddle. Like most big horses, the shire is gentle and easy to handle, which makes a ride on its back a pleasure. Of course, it is also exciting to be a part of its tremendous power.

CHAPTER 4

All About Ponies

In This Chapter

➤ Details about ponies

➤ Taking care of ponies

➤ The most popular breeds

In this chapter, you'll learn all about ponies. You'll learn about the physical characteristics that make them unique, how to feed and care for them, and which pony breeds are the most popular along with their many individual characteristics.

Modern Ponies

The smallest of the equines, ponies often bring a smile to the face because they are so adorable. But most ponies have a long tradition of work in their native countries. Through the centuries, they were used in places where bigger horses couldn't fit. They also could carry loads with more efficiency than many of the bigger animals.

Today, ponies, especially the smaller ones, are the ideal size for children. Most have a friendly demeanor and enjoy attention. They also do not require as much space in their stall as bigger horses require, and that makes it easier to care for them.

Pony Facts

For most equine registries, a pony is not supposed to be higher than 14.2 hands, though this may vary by breed and country. Some horses are classified as ponies just by tradition, or because the heritage of their breeding was made up of ponies. Certain breeds are still classified as ponies because their conformation resembles that of a pony rather than a horse.

There are other differences between ponies and larger horses besides their height. Since most of the breeds come from northern territories, the ponies often have heavier coats. Their manes and their tails in particular are usually quite thick. Their legs tend to be proportionately shorter, while their necks look thicker and more powerful.

Ponies are generally heartier than bigger equines. Considering their size, ponies also have more strength than larger horses. Their compact build can generate plenty of power. Ponies also tend to have fewer health problems than full-sized horses.

Because of their size, ponies often get treated more like household pets. Generally, they respond with a good deal of affection to the attention, but on occasion, they have also been known to be more stubborn and mischievous than larger horses.

Taking Care of a Pony

Ponies have certain requirements to ensure their safety. As with a full-sized horse, you can keep a pony in a yard, but you'll need to have lower fencing. Because of its smaller size, a pony can slip under a fence if the lowest barriers are too high off the ground. Ponies can also slip between panels higher up if there is too much space.

It's also important to check and clean a pony's feet more frequently than you would for a larger horse. A pony's feet are even more delicate than a full-sized horse's feet, so they need constant attention.

Feeding a Pony

Another way ponies differ from all other horses is in the way they eat. They do not need as much food and they do not need to eat as often as horses do. Even after you make adjustments for their size, ponies do not need as many calories.

The type of food that ponies eat is also somewhat different. They generally only need hay derived from grass. Alfalfa hay is not necessary. Horses eat 20 pounds or more of hay a day, whereas ponies need only 10 pounds of hay a day, if that.

A pony also does not need to graze the way most horses do. Lush grass can actually make a pony ill. Because of their delicate digestive systems, they are at risk of getting the deadly equine diseases of colic and laministis if they eat grasses too rich in sugars. Ponies should not be allowed to graze for more than a few minutes.

Pony Breeds

Most of the pony breeds are ancient, going back hundreds of years. But there are also newer breeds created by pony enthusiasts that combine crosses of other horses.

Some ponies continue to live in the wild, many of them off the shores of America. Their ancestors were among the many horses brought to North and South America by the Spanish in the sixteenth century.

Horse Sense

Many of the breeds of pony that survive today developed in harsh northern lands, where there was little food. The Shetland pony, for instance, developed on the moors of Scotland, where the amount of food available was quite limited. The Shetland and many other breeds did not have access to the grasses that bigger horses thrived on.

Banker

The banker is derived from Spanish horses brought to the Americas in the sixteenth century. They began living in the wild and eventually settled in on the Atlantic shore. They reside along the marshes and banks of North Carolina, where their habitat is protected by the government.

The banker's numbers are monitored, and some of them are put up for adoption each year. Bankers that have been domesticated have proven to be good riding horses. Among ponies, they are well known for their powerful stride and good movement. They are also quite gentle and friendly, which makes them an excellent choice for children to ride.

Like many ponies, the body of the banker is small yet sturdy with bones that are quite strong. They are known for their heartiness and good health. Their height ranges from 13 hands to 14.3 hands. The weight of a banker can range from 800 to 1,000 pounds.

Chincoteague Pony

This breed developed from wild ponies that lived along the Atlantic coast near Maryland and Virginia. They are still allowed to roam through the shore areas in those states. They are generally undisturbed, other than for some peaceful control of their numbers. The Chincoteague are fairly small ponies, usually reaching heights between 13 and 13.2 hands in the wild.

To keep control of the population totals, some of the Chincoteague, like the banker ponies, are taken off their home island and sold for adoption. Once they are domesticated and provided with better and more consistent feedings, they usually grow bigger, to over 14 hands high.

Connemara

The breeds of ponies most popular in the world come from areas of the United Kingdom. The Connemara is another example of this. It was developed in Ireland, though it is now bred throughout the world. Its history is similar to the Scottish and Welsh ponies since it is a breed that developed and survived in harsh conditions.

In appearance, the Connemara is quite different from most other ponies, since its features are well defined. Other than its size, the Connemara looks more like a full-sized horse than any other pony. Its movements are also more graceful than those of most ponies. It is often seen in the show ring since it is well-known for its jumping ability.

Fjord

The fjord is usually considered a pony, but most members of the breed are above the 14.2 hands threshold. Many weigh over 1,000 pounds as well.

The fjord pony is from Norway. It is one of the few ponies that features a specific color. All members of the breed are the tan or gold color called dun. If a fjord is not a dun color, it cannot become a member of the registry.

The fjord is one of the oldest known breeds in the equine world. Its history can be traced back close to 4,000 years. The breed is strong enough that it can be used for extensive field work, but it is small enough and kind enough to be ridden by children. It is also one of the breeds used most often by disabled riders.

Haflinger

Many haflingers are too tall to be classified as a pony, with many of the breed growing beyond the 14.2-hands limit. These ponies were developed in the mountainous region that connects northern Italy to Austria. The breed can be traced back many centuries and, despite having been in the middle of a number of major military conflicts, the haflinger has survived into the twenty-first century.

The breed is still considered to be a pony, though that designation may not last for long. The leading breeders of haflinger stock are trying hard to increase the size of the breed.

The haflinger is a good-moving horse. It is often seen these days at western riding events.

Pony of the Americas

This breed was developed in the state of Iowa during the 1950s. All members of the breed must have the coloring of an Appaloosa, one of the foundation breeds of the Pony of the Americas, along with the Arabian and the Shetland pony. The members of the breed tend to be quite tall for ponies, as high as 14 hands.

The Pony of the Americas breed is quite successful in hunt seat competitions, including three-day Eventing, which combines Dressage, racing and jumping. eventing. This is not surprising because the breed has become known for its stamina.

Shetland Pony

The Shetland can be a really small animal. Its height can range from as little as 7 hands up to a still not very high 11 hands. But what it lacks in height, it makes up for in toughness and determination.

The Shetland pony was developed in the harsh conditions of Scotland. Its coat is thick to offer protection from the elements. It also has a thick mane, which serves the same purpose as its coat. Its body, in particular the neck, is strong and sturdy; its legs are short and powerful.

The American version of the Shetland is somewhat more refined. It is not quite as stout and the hair of its coat is not as heavy as the Scottish Shetland.

In the past, Shetland ponies were often put to work. They were used to carry loads appropriate for their size. They were also used in coal mines, where the space is quite limited. Most all these jobs no longer exist.

Shetlands are great with children. They are usually just the right size for a small child to get on board without much trouble. Shetlands are also very easy to steer from a cart.

Among all the ponies, the Shetland is usually considered the most popular.

Riding Vocab

A cob is a small horse, just slightly larger than a pony. This at least helps to explains why the Welsh cob is traditionally listed as a pony, even though it isn't one.

The Welsh Ponies

There are a variety of ponies that come under the Welsh heading. They are broken down by height and type. There is the Welsh mountain pony, which is the smallest of the group, between 12 and 12.2 hands high. Slightly bigger is the breed known specifically as the Welsh pony, also known as the Welsh Pony of riding type. Next is the Welsh pony of cob type, and the biggest of all is the Welsh cob, which can be ridden by both adults and children.

Like the Shetland pony, the Welsh ponies are all hardy and sturdy, also raised to deal with a harsh climate. They look more like a full-sized horse than the Shetland (which looks more like a squashed horse.)

The Welsh pony has a long list of uses in Wales, including work on behalf of the military. You won't find it in battle anymore, but you will see it in the show ring, competing in various equestrian competitions.

Grade Ponies

Grade ponies are similar to grade horses. Their breeding is either unknown, or they are simply not purebreds. But as with grade horses, grade ponies can still make good pets. They make great companions and can also be good ponies for learning young riders.

PART TWO

Getting Started

CHAPTER 5

Riding Options

> **In This Chapter**
>
> ➤ Deciding what you want
> ➤ Examining your options
> ➤ Choosing your course
> ➤ Riding for the impaired

Your love for horses has given you the desire to become a rider, but you're not sure what to do next. In this chapter, you'll learn about the activities that are available when you become involved in the world of horses. You'll learn about the different types of riding traditions that you can pursue, the horse sports in which you can participate, and what to do to get started and involved in the highly enjoyable world of riding horses.

You'll also learn about the riding opportunities available for the physically and mentally impaired.

Do I Even Need Lessons?

Unless you already know how to ride, the answer to this question is yes. The first consideration has to be for your safety. Maybe you can figure out how to swim by just being tossed into the pool, although that's questionable. But it is much too dangerous to try to ride a horse if you don't know what you're doing. If you have no training and get on a horse, you could be endangering many more people than yourself.

Here is what you need to know before you start riding:

➤ The safety requirements of riding

➤ How to put gear on a horse and how it works

➤ How to get on a horse safely

➤ How to get your horse moving

➤ How to steer a horse and get him to make turns

➤ The various ways the horse moves

➤ How to get a horse to stop safely

For these reasons, among others, you need lessons. If a friend or family member wants to instruct you, make sure he knows what he's doing.

Horse Sense

A riding academy provides horses that are proven less likely to be bothered by new riders. If you're trying to learn how to ride from inexperienced instructors, you have no way of knowing if the horse you get on is going to be cooperative or even safe for you to ride.

Understanding Your Options

When you decide to take lessons, the first thing you need to do is determine what type of riding you want to learn. There are many different types of riding that you can pursue, so you'll need to decide which one is right for you. Almost all of the activities of horses and riders are broken down into two categories—English and western.

English Riding

English riding includes all the sports and activities developed in the United Kingdom, primarily in the nineteenth century. Some of them trace to games played in distant countries of the British Empire. Many others trace to British-based riding traditions developed for fox hunting. They feature the type of equipment developed for leaping over fences and other obstacles, as well as gallops over the uneven and grassy terrains of the English countryside.

There are plenty of more peaceful and popular ways of riding that have evolved from fox hunting, including jumping and cross-country riding. There are other disciplines that show off the training of the horse and the skill of the rider. These English sports include dressage, in which horses are rated as they go through many designated steps, and equitation, which rates the rider's ability to control his horse.

The tack used in English riding (tack being the horseman's word for equipment) is designed to promote the flexibility of the horse and not so much the comfort of the rider. The saddles are usually lightweight and easy to carry. They are also not that complicated, with a limited number of parts to attach.

English Competitions

There are a number of sports that come under the heading of English riding. Hunt seat events—which no longer involve hunting—include show jumping and cross-country racing. They are combined with dressage in a three-day competition known as eventing. If you take lessons in English riding, you can learn how to ride in any or all of these events.

Another sport that is considered part of the English riding tradition is polo. This is a sport that British soldiers learned from the locals in Asia, and then spread throughout the world. Though there are some other forms of the sport, the horses and riders in the most popular form of polo—the one played on a large field with a mallet and a ball—utilize English riding equipment.

If you're interested in polo, there are plenty of academies that will not only teach you how to ride if you're a beginner, but will also teach you the rules of the game and how to play it.

Western Riding

Like English riding, most western riding activities come from the nineteenth century. They are based on the traditions of the American West. Many of these traditions came from the Mexican riders known as the vaqueros who had previously roamed those areas as well as the regions further to the south.

Western riders often rode long distances over dry desert land. They needed to be able to carry a lot of supplies with them in order to survive and to take care of their horses. As a result, their saddles needed to be bigger and sturdier than those used by English riders. They were carrying more gear and they needed the saddle to be larger and more comfortable.

Riding Vocab

Vaquero translated from the Spanish means cowboy or cow-herder.

The saddle and other gear used by a western rider also had to be sturdy to deal with the jobs of the cowboy. The saddle had to be strong enough so that another animal could be tied to the horn. The saddle also had to be designed so that a rider could get off the horse quickly after roping a steer, for example.

The traditional work activities of western riders and cowboys are still utilized on some ranches, but most of them have now evolved into western sports. There are many popular events that have now been grouped together and are performed in competitions at rodeos and other western events. These include such sports as calf and steer roping and herding sports such as penning and cutting.

Another western sport is barrel racing, which displays a horse's speed and turning ability. There are other competitions that show off a horse's stride and discipline, such as western pleasure and reining.

Western-style riding instruction teaches you all the features and traditions of the West. You'll learn about the specific and often colorful gear used for western riding, including the headstall bridles and the large saddles. You'll also learn how to handle the reins in a western style. What's more, most of the stables that offer western riding lessons can get you involved with the most popular western sports, particularly barrel racing.

Choosing an Activity

There are a lot of different activities you can pursue as a rider. All of the sports, whether they are English or western, welcome new riders and have programs that help get them involved. This is especially true for young people. Every type of riding discipline has a youth program to develop new riders under the age of eighteen.

Even if have already decided on the kind of riding or riding style you want to pursue, you might change your mind when you consider all the options available. But there are other factors that can influence your decision. For instance, the training you're seeking may not be offered in your area.

Equine Tip

If you're living in a warm climate and have no preference for the riding style you'd like to learn, you might want to choose English riding instruction. The English riding gear is a lot lighter and will be more comfortable in hot conditions than the much heavier western gear.

Western riding lessons are pretty easy to find west of the Mississippi and particularly west of the Rockies. They are also readily available in the southwest and other areas where rodeos are popular. But if you live on the East Coast, you will probably have a harder time finding an academy that will teach you how to ride western-style.

Wherever you are, you'll probably be able to find a place that can teach you the basics of dressage and jumping. These activities are popular almost everywhere. The fact that they are the featured events of Olympic equestrian events also increases their popularity.

Choosing a Horse

What kind of a horse do you want to ride? Are you a smaller person who is going to be comfortable riding a pony? Perhaps you've been given a horse, or a family member or friend has one. Then the decision as to what kind of horse you want to ride has been made for you.

You may decide to choose a type of horse based on stables or academies in your area that offer more specialized kinds of lessons. There are places where you can learn to ride a certain type of horse, for instance, including ones with fancy strides, such as the Tennessee walking horse or the Missouri fox trotter.

If you're lucky, you'll be able to choose a horse that meets the specific needs of the type of riding you want to learn to do. Do some research, talk to professional horse people, gather all the information you can to help you decide.

Do not be hasty. Choosing the type of horse you want to ride is a big decision, so don't rush into it.

Your Commitment

You can pursue riding casually or you can take it more seriously. You don't have to decide this before you start, but eventually, you'll need to make this decision.

You might want to compete in shows. Most every type of riding offers events for new riders. They may be called novice or beginner events, but by any name, the idea is to develop riders so that eventually they can compete in competition at higher levels.

Financial and Time Constraints

Before you start, make sure you can handle the expenses of riding. Lessons are not that cheap, about $100 an hour or more. Of course, if you're planning on buying a horse, there are even more costs.

Even if the expenses are not a problem, there are also time considerations. Chances are you don't have unlimited time available for lessons, so before you start or make a commitment, make sure you know how much time you can devote to riding.

Riding for the Impaired

A disability does not always prevent you from riding. There are many facilities that offer riding for adults and children with physical and mental challenges.

For those battling their limitations, the opportunity to ride a horse offers great therapy. They can improve self-esteem while developing personal confidence.

Besides the psychological advantages of riding for the impaired, there can be some real physical advantages. In particular, riding can help stretch legs and improve balance and coordination.

The facilities that offer riding for the physically challenged will have the appropriate gentle horses for the assignment as well as specialized instructors. The rider is secured in the saddle before the lesson begins. Normally, the teacher leads the horse around by a rope attached to a noseband, or cavesson.

Paralympics

If you continue to pursue a riding career with your disability, some day you might be good enough to compete in the Paralympics equestrian events. Those are events for riders sixteen and older, in which the competitions are divided by the type of impairment of the rider.

The lone event is dressage, or as it's called in the competition, para dressage. Para dressage is similar to dressage, but the moves are appropriate for the condition of the riders. Extra aids, including audio aids for visually impaired riders, are allowed to help the riders compete.

Metals are awarded to the individual winners, and team awards are given as well.

Ready to Go

You've made up your mind. You know what kind of riding you want or are capable of doing. The next step is to get lessons.

CHAPTER 6

Finding a Riding Facility

In This Chapter

➤ Finding a facility

➤ Final decision

➤ Lessons for children

In this chapter, you'll learn how to turn your desire to ride into reality. You'll learn how to find the riding facility that is the best fit for what you want to do and the steps you should take before deciding where to do your riding.

You'll discover the most important questions to ask and learn about the various options you should look for in a riding facility.

You'll learn about adult riding camps and all the extras that they can offer, as well as what to expect when it comes to your costs for learning to ride and taking part in the sport.

You'll also learn about lessons for children—when to start them, what they will entail, and how much they will cost.

Location

You've decided to pursue your dream of riding a horse, but you don't know where to go. This shouldn't be a problem, because no matter where you are in the country, you're likely to find a place nearby where you can learn how to ride. There are well over a thousand riding academies in the United States offering lessons.

The best source is word of mouth. Find out if someone you know can recommend a good riding facility. The next step is to look in the phone book and on the Internet.

How Much Time Do You Have?

Before you decide where to go, you should first figure out the amount of time that you have or can devote to riding. That includes the time commuting to a farm or stable. If you have just one day a week when you have time to ride, say late on a Friday afternoon, do you also have the time to commute to the location? Is it convenient for public transportation, or do you have to drive there? And even if all those issues are not problems, does the facility have availability when you're ready to ride or is it booked solidly at those hours?

Most riding locations say you should set aside two hours for your lesson. The actual lesson usually is less than an hour, but almost all riding academies want you to learn more than just how to ride. They want you to know how to take care of your horse before you get on his back.

Normally, a program for lessons last about two months, but some riding academies will allow you to join a class at any time, provided that there are still openings in the program.

Stables have only a certain number of horses and trainers, so it may be necessary to make your reservation in advance, possibly well in advance, of the time of the lessons. Also, find out when you have to pay for the lessons and when you'll need to pay once you've started riding.

Some facilities let you book only a month or two ahead. Others may be taking reservations for a time way ahead of that. You need to know all of that information. You'll also need to know how much of a deposit you have to make before you begin your lessons.

The Facility

The riding academy you choose needs to be conveniently located, have hours that meet your schedule, and offer the kind of lessons you want.

The Lessons

Find out what kind of riding the academy is teaching. Does it offer training for English riding activities, such as jumping and dressage, or does it prepare riders for western-style events such as barrel racing? Most academies have one approach, but not both.

You may also have your mind set on riding a certain type of horse, be it an Arabian or a Clydesdale or something else. On their websites, most riding facilities list the breeds they have available.

You can look for places to ride by searching for academies that offer the specific breed you're looking for. Whatever search engine you're using, key in the breed and your location and several choices are likely to be available. Type something like "quarter horse riding lessons California," and you'll get plenty of options to explore.

Some academies specialize in training novices to ride horses with fancier strides, such as Missouri fox trotters or Tennessee walking horses. They will show you how to get the horse into these elegant and unusual steps.

Usually, the facilities of these stables are similar to other riding academies, and the lessons are about the same length. It's just that they offer a specialized type of riding, and they have their horses trained and raised for a particular style.

If you are a rider who has previous experience but you want to learn more, or if you haven't ridden for a while and want a refresher course, most academies offer advanced riding classes. Riders are placed in classes based on their level of riding skill so academies will be able to find a class that's appropriate for you.

The riding facility will teach you the proper way to brush your horse as well as put on a saddle and a bridle. It will also teach you how to take care of your horse after riding, taking off the gear (untacking), cooling out the horse, and then grooming him before he is put back in his stall.

Most academies will want you to reach a minimum level of riding accomplishment before they advance you to their next level of instruction. Some academies want you not only to be able to perform basic moves on a horse before they'll advance you, but also to demonstrate that you can perform these moves on more than one horse.

The Instructors

Try to find out about the people who'll be teaching you. The stable's website should list the qualifications of its instructors. This doesn't quite work like a college, where the college degrees of each professor are listed, but there are plenty of facts available, such as:

➤ How long has the instructor been teaching?

➤ How long has the instructor been at this facility?

➤ What type of riding career has the instructor had?

➤ What other horse-related credentials, such as an equine studies degree or a veterinary degree, does the instructor have?

Viewing the Facility

Some facilities have DVDs showcasing their stables and schools that are available for prospective customers or on their websites. If you watch a DVD and are impressed enough to make more inquiries and get a tour of the facility, make sure that what you're seeing before your eyes matches what you saw on the video presentation.

Touring the Facility

When you're given a tour of a stable, look the place over closely. You want everything to look immaculate. You want the fences to be painted, you want the paths to be clear, and you want the barns to be clean. If a stable, especially one that is trying to get your money for lessons, does not take good care of its whole facility, there's no reason for you to be associated with it.

Don't forget that riding a horse, though it's a lot of fun and can provide great enjoyment and satisfaction, is also a potentially dangerous activity. Especially if you're new to riding, you'll be relying on someone else's expertise to keep you safe. For instance, you'll have to assume that the saddles are safe and not worn and that the helmets have been inspected.

A riding stable probably won't be in business too long if the place is poorly run and injuries and other problems begin to add up. But you don't want to be the last one injured at a barn before it gets closed down.

It's all right to ask a lot of questions about these matters. If you see anything out of sorts, do not hesitate to ask. Why is that bucket laying over there? Why is that light not working? Why does that horse seem to be upset? These are the type of questions you would need answered.

It doesn't matter that the place is the most convenient for you or that the hours are right or that your teenager is making a fuss wanting to get lessons. Your safety or your family member's safety is most important.

Equine Tip

Find out if the stable has indoor air conditioning. Many farms do not have this, and for the amount of money you're paying for lessons, you may want some extra comfort, especially if you're riding on a hot day. Most riding academies want you to learn how to groom your horse and put on his saddle and bridle before you ride, so you'll be spending a good deal of time inside before you go out on your horse.

The lack of air conditioning around the barn can be a problem for the horses. Especially if you're a new rider, your lesson is likely to be affected if your horse is sweating quite a bit.

Key Questions to Ask

Find out how many extra fees might be tacked on to your costs. Find out if the fee for the riding lesson includes the equipment, such as riding gear and helmet, or if there is a separate fee to rent them as well as the saddle and bridle. Some academies add other charges, such as for an extra handler assigned to the horse. This kind of charge is especially prevalent when you buy lessons for a youngster.

You're the one putting up the money, so there are important matters to know before you start:

> ➤ Does the stable decide the times and days of the lesson, or do you?

> ➤ Are the lessons all private or all group, and if they are group lessons, how many are in a group?

Some academies list their lessons as being semiprivate, which is a term apparently borrowed from the health care industry. If you've been in a hospital room, you know that a semiprivate room isn't particularly private. You may not want semiprivate lessons, unless you're bringing along a family member or friend with whom you want to share the experience.

You may be willing to pay more for private lessons. Not all riding academies will offer them, so find this out before you get yourself emotionally committed to a stable.

Other riding academies begin their program with private lessons. Usually, the private lessons are shorter, probably a half hour, whereas the semiprivate or small group lessons go on for an hour.

Equine Tip

Year-round lessons are possible throughout some areas of America, but other areas are seasonal because of the weather. Academies that operate seasonally have specific dates for their programs, and you'll need to join at the beginning the program.

Some academies in colder climates have created indoor riding facilities, which allow them to offer lessons year-round. Though that might not be what you're looking for, it's likely to be the only option available in winter climates.

The Final Decision

Once you've narrowed your choice of facility down to a few, you'll want to ask specific questions and meet with the people you'll be dealing with. The first one is the person who is actually running the place, whether he is the owner or the barn manager.

Naturally, you want that person to be friendly and considerate. As you discuss the prospects of signing up with his facility, you don't want him acting like he's doing you a favor by letting you ride his horses.

If the person in charge passes this test, then go on to discuss what you're looking for from your riding. No doubt he (or she) has already heard every reason a potential new client has for wanting to ride. The barn manager should be able to explain your options for instruction, the fees, the weekly schedule, and the length of the courses.

Not only will you want to know the costs, but you'll also want to know what kind of deals you can get. If you book more lessons, will you get a better price? Find out if other benefits are offered, such as discounts for clothing or other riding-related items.

You'll want to know if the facility has safe places to put your valuables while you're riding. You don't necessarily want to bring all of them with you when you're in the barn or the riding ring. You'll want to see where you can keep them. Don't be afraid to ask other questions, such as whether the farm offers Wi-Fi for your mobile device.

You also want to check parking availability. You might have been given a nice spot for your preview, but find out if you'll be able to park that close once your lessons begin.

Taking Another Tour

After your discussion with the manager, you should have him show you around the place. You probably toured the facility before, but the manager will be able to explain a lot more. On this tour, you'll be doing more than just checking out the looks of the place. You'll also want to know where you'll be going to be with your horse before you ride him, and you'll also want to see where you'll be going once you get on his back.

Check out the riding rings. If you're at a large facility with much bigger paddocks or even trails used for the lessons, check them out, too. Make sure these places are maintained properly. You'll be riding your horse over them, and you should expect them to be cared for properly.

Meeting the Instructors

You'll want to talk to the people who would be giving you your actual training. Obviously, just like the manager, you want the trainers to be friendly and receptive. It's even more important that you like these folks since they're the ones you'll be dealing with during your lessons.

Ask the instructors about the horses in the barn. Find out what breeds are available and how experienced they are working as training horses. Have the trainer introduce you to them. Get to know them a little. Let the trainer tell you a little more about each horse, including his personality.

While the trainer is taking you through the barn, you can again check over the facility. Again, even if you've looked over the place before and were satisfied, you're probably getting a closer look at the stalls and other parts of the barn. Plus, if you've looked over some other farms in the meantime, you might have noticed other things you want to check for, such as the tack room. Also, look for safety equipment such as fire extinguishers and smoke alarms. If you don't see them, keep asking questions.

Your Choice

If you're satisfied with everything you've seen, sign yourself up. But if you have any doubts and there were other facilities that were almost as convenient and offering just about what you want, you may want to check them out, or check them out again.

In the end, where you or your family members will get riding lessons is an important decision. You're not only going to devote a lot of time learning to ride, but you're also going to be spending a fair amount of money. More than that, you may be giving you or a loved one a highly enjoyable lifetime activity. So take your time and be comfortable with your decision.

Riding Camps

While many of the riding camps around the country are for youths only, there are also camps established for adults. They offer everything you can get from a riding academy and more. The lessons are longer, the options are greater, and the experience should be even more memorable.

Camps are also arranged in the same manner as academies, with divisions for amateur on up to advanced rider training. At some locations, the camps are also divided by age, including groups for seniors.

Some of the places are just day camps, in which you come in for the day or have an overnight stay. There are others that have a program for a week of more.

You'll live in the environment of a farm or ranch. You'll be around horses all day. You'll be getting more than lessons; you'll be interacting with the horses, caring for them, and feeding them treats.

Since you'll be there all day, there will be time for more than just basic lessons. At many camps, bareback riding is offered. You also might go for a moonlight ride. You could also hear some interesting lectures on various horse subjects.

There are some camps that are set up for whole families to attend. Adults can be riding in a program while the children are off getting lessons of their own.

In addition to riding lessons and horse-related activities for all, there are usually many non-riding activities scheduled as well. Depending on the location, there could be trips offered to popular tourist spots. Northern California camps, for instance, usually offer tours of the wine country.

Dude Ranches

In a western camp, or dude ranch, there are plenty of other things to do. You can learn how to throw a lasso or you can work with cattle. There's also plenty of time and opportunity for trail riding.

At a dude ranch, there is usually a campfire set up in the evening, with some old ranch hand reciting old cowboy legends. The whole experience can provide you with an authentic feel of the old West, without losing many of the modern conveniences.

Camp Costs

Riding camps are naturally more expensive than just lessons, though not that much. Depending on the facility, a day in a day camp can cost anywhere from $100 on up, whereas a week at a camp can be over $1,000. Of course, you can search the Internet looking for the best prices. Most camps require a deposit to secure your spot in a program. Programs are usually limited and seasonal.

Children's Lessons

The procedure for picking a place to get lessons for your child is not that much different from the way you decide where to get lessons for yourself, with some obvious differences. Your children are reliant on you to put them in a safe place, so you'll need to take the same approach you would use when picking a school for them, again with some obvious differences. When you check the facility over, not to mention the people running the place and giving lessons, you'll want to do it very carefully, since it is your child.

The main concern has to be for their safety. Not just the normal concerns for their well-being and protection, but also for their safety during their lessons. You have to know the equipment is safe. Make sure the helmets being used are certified. Also make sure the horses are an appropriate size for your children.

Teaching Young People

Most facilities will not begin lessons for children until they reach either age six or seven. They consider it too frustrating to deal with kids that are any younger than that because of their short attention span.

You can probably find a place where children six or under can get on a pony to ride without getting lessons. There are other places, such as petting zoos, where children can be around horses and ponies. If they like these experiences enough, they are likely to ask for lessons when they get to be old enough.

The lessons for children are usually about a half-hour long. As with adults, the initial lessons are private to allow for more direct instruction. As the child progresses, assuming that the boy or girl continues to be interested, the lessons can be lengthened to an hour and may be changed to a group setting.

Children will also learn about taking care of a horse. Even though they won't yet be taught how to put all of the equipment on the horse, they will begin to practice gentle brushing of the horse and other light activities.

Costs

Lessons for children are not usually as expensive as they are for adults. They range from $25 to $50 per half-hour lesson, depending on the location, among other things. You may also need to buy a helmet, which costs close to $200, and boots, which are probably less than $50.

You probably don't need to be reminded that children, especially young ones, can change their minds and lose interest in something quickly. So be careful how much of a financial commitment you're making. Buying a good deal of expensive gear or making long-term commitments for lessons will seem a very bad investment if your youngster decides after a couple of weeks that he is no longer interested and won't go to his lesson.

Benefits

It's possible your child might lose interest in riding, but it's more likely that he will enjoy it and want to keep getting better and learning more. Getting children to start riding at a young age gives them an activity they can enjoy for a lifetime. As they learn how to handle and care for a horse, they learn about responsibility. They also make friends with fellow young riders that will help them develop a better sense of cooperation.

CHAPTER 7

Halters and Bridles

In This Chapter

➤ How to put on a halter

➤ Different parts of a bridle

➤ Western headstalls

In this chapter, you'll learn about the key pieces of equipment that you'll need to control your horse. You'll learn about halters and how to put them on correctly, as well as the various types of bridles and the pieces that they contain. You'll also learn about the many bridle variations used by western riders, who refer to them as headstalls.

The Halter

At first glance you might not be able to tell if what a horse is wearing is a bridle or a halter because they both fit around the head and can look quite similar. But a halter is designed to be used when you're leading or walking the horse, whereas the bridle is designed to control the horse when you're riding him.

A halter has a strap called the crownpiece that lies across the top of the horse's head. There is also a noseband that goes across the face. The two pieces are connected.

Make sure that the pieces are the right size. You will need to adjust the straps for your horse. An ill-fitting halter can leave marks on a horse's face and be uncomfortable.

Halters are sold based on the horse's height. They are also sold by the breed, such as a pony halter or an Arabian halter.

Most halters these days have a buckle and a ring that connect and secure the two parts. There are other halters that are made only of rope and do not have any metal. They need to be tied together in a knot, usually a double knot.

Putting on the Halter

The halter is designed to be tied or buckled on the left side of the horse. You're going to be leading the horse from that side, so the attachment to connect the two parts of the halter and the lead rope needs to be on the left. Usually, there is a loop or buckle on the other side in case you need to tie or cross tie the horse from the right.

The safest way to put a halter on a horse is from the top down. Begin by putting the crownpiece under the horse's neck with your left hand. Then reach over his neck to grab the piece on his other side with your right hand.

Horse Sense

When putting on the halter, you're just asking for trouble if you put on the noseband first. You'll then be forced to either pull the crownpiece across your horse's face or throw the straps up to your hand at the top of his head. You're liable to hit him in the eye or ear or cause some other problem when you try to do it in those ways.

If these wrong-headed moves end up hurting your horse, he will resent you for it and be mad at you, as he should be.

Horse Sense

After being haltered a few times, your horse will get used to putting his nose into the noseband, so he shouldn't object. He'll know that you're going to lead him around safely, and the two of you will be going out to have fun.

Before you secure the crownpiece, lift the noseband up into the right position over the horse's nose and above his mouth. Then stretch the crownpiece across the poll, or top of his head, until it is in place. Pull the straps of the two pieces together on the left side of the horse's head. Fasten the crownpiece into the noseband buckle or ring. The lead rope, which will be 10 to 15 feet long, usually attaches onto the same ring.

For some horses that are harder to control or more powerful, an extra attachment, such as a chain, might be added to the rope. A different kind of halter is used to do this, one that includes an extra attachment either over the nose or under the chin.

Bridles and Headstalls

While a halter is used to control a horse when you're walking him, a bridle or a headstall is used when you're on his back. A bridle is the term used by English-style riders, while headstall is the name used by Western riders. There are differences in designs between a bridle and a headstall, but they have the same purpose.

Don't think of the bridle or the headstall as just a piece of equipment, because it is also a communication device. Stop, go, faster, slower, left, right—the primary way that all of these and other signals come to the horse is through the bridle.

The English Bridle

The English bridle, known as a snaffle bridle, looks quite a bit like a halter. It also has a crownpiece at the top and a noseband, but there is a browband that lies across the top of the face, under the ears. There are also cheekpieces that run down the sides of the horse's face and connect to the various parts. A throatlatch is also used under the horse's jaw to help keep the other pieces in place.

Bridle Sizes

Bridles come in three standard sizes:

1. Pony: Fits horses—or, more appropriately, ponies—up to about 14 hands

2. Cob: Fits horses from 14 to 16 hands

3. Full-size: Fits larger horses

These measurements assume that your horse has a head that is a normal size for his height. If you need to, keep changing the bridle until you get the right size.

It's important that the bridle fits your horse correctly. If you don't get the right size and the horse is uncomfortable, he'll be fighting you and won't cooperate. The mouthpiece needs to go into his mouth comfortably. The straps should not be pulling on the bit, or it's possible that the pieces may become detached.

Bits and Other Pieces

The bit is the most important part of the snaffle bridle. It consists of a mouthpiece connected to rings that sit outside the mouth on either side. None of the other parts of the bridle will have any effect if the bit is not set properly and does not fit your horse.

If the bit is too thin, it will pinch the horse's mouth; if it's too big, it will not have any effect. The standard size of a bit is 5 inches. Usually, only the very large warm-blooded horses will need a bit larger than that. Ponies and some smaller breeds will take a smaller size, either 4½ inches or 4¾ inches.

Bits are made of many different materials. Most mouthpieces are made of metal, and the best and most expensive ones are made of stainless steel. There are softer yet still sturdy bits made of vulcanized metal or rubber. These are designed for horses with very sensitive or damaged mouths.

Do not try to improve your horse's behavior by making the bit more severe so as to increase your power or control over him. The horse will not become more cooperative by punishing him or making him suffer.

If you're using a snaffle bit, you should get used to controlling your horse's head from side to side, which is how the snaffle bit is designed to work. Do not pull the horse's head back by yanking on both reins at the same time. That is the way a bit that uses leverage works. That will not work well with a snaffle bit.

Types of Snaffle Bit

There are many different kinds of snaffle bits. The variations are in the mouthpiece and the ring attachments. The mouthpiece can have a straight bar or have a joint in the middle. The separation of the mouthpiece is designed for greater comfort of the horse.

The rings can be various round shapes and can be joined in the middle or in a link. The various types of snaffle bits include the following:

➤ Standard snaffle bit, which has round rings

➤ Eggbutt bit, which has oval-shaped rings with the mouthpiece attached

➤ French Link snaffle bit, with a mouthpiece that has two connected parts

➤ D-ring bit, which is in the shape of a D

Putting on the Snaffle Bridle

The first few times you put a snaffle bridle on a horse, you should have an experienced horse person to guide and assist you. But here are the steps you will need to take.

Most of the parts of the bridle should already be fastened and in place before you put it on a horse. Make sure the browband and the noseband are both straight and not drooping because it will be difficult to get them adjusted once the bridle is on the horse's face.

Riding Vocab

A D-ring on a bridle is spelled with just the letter, but there is a similarly shaped and named attachment to a western saddle, which is called a Dee ring.

Do not try to put on the bridle until you have control of the horse. When you're ready to begin, take off the halter. Then loop the reins around the horse's neck. Throughout the process of putting on the bridle, always keep the end of the reins around your hand. This will prevent you from losing control of the horse should he start to move.

There are different ways to put on the bridle, but perhaps the best procedure begins by you putting your right hand between the horse's ears at the top of his head with the crownpiece in your hand. Then pull the rest of the bridle low enough so that the mouthpiece hangs below his mouth. Be careful not to hit him with the bridle.

Putting on the Mouthpiece

While you continue to hold the top of the bridle with your right hand, use your left hand to lift up the mouthpiece into the horse's mouth. The bit fits into the mouth at the bars, the open areas on both sides of the jaw where the horse has no teeth.

Next, lift the whole bridle up by the crownpiece until the horse takes in the mouthpiece and it is securely in place. Do all of this gently as the horse's mouth and teeth are both sensitive.

When properly placed, the mouthpiece faces forward in the horse's mouth. You can tell if it is in correctly if it creates a couple of wrinkles on his lips. If it doesn't, it means the bit is too loose and won't function. Too many wrinkles, and it's too tight.

There should be enough room between the rings of the bit and the horse's mouth for your finger.

Putting on the Crownpiece and the Browband

Next, put the crownpiece in place high on the horse's head. Pull it over his ears one at a time. Again, do this gently because the skin around a horse's ears is also very sensitive.

Then position the browband below the horse's ears, high on his forehead. If the browband is too tight, it will pull on the crownpiece and put pressure on the horse's sensitive ears. If it's too loose, it won't stay in place.

Putting on the Noseband

The next step is to put on the noseband, which, as on a halter, stretches across the face parallel to the browband. Despite its name, the noseband does not touch the nose but needs to be above it and all the surrounding cartilage. It also needs to be high enough on the face so the horse can open his mouth freely.

The noseband is secured by fastening the strap into the appropriate places on the cheekpieces. Do not leave any leather ends hanging. Make sure everything is secure.

You should also be able to get a finger under the noseband. Don't make it any tighter unless you know that your horse either tends to open his mouth too much or gets his tongue over the bit. Then you could try tightening the noseband a bit to see if that will solve the problem.

Riding Vocab

The problems caused by horses that open their mouth too often are also addressed by an item known as a drop noseband. It is placed lower on a horse's face, though still clear of the mouth.

Another piece of equipment that deals with this is called a flash noseband. It is attached near the noseband and hangs a little lower toward the mouth.

Yet another attachment that is designed for this problem is called a figure eight noseband, though it looks more like an X than an 8. It's used primarily to keep the mouth closed on jumping horses.

Putting on the Throatlatch

The final move is to put on the throatlatch, which goes under and around the horse's jaw. It attaches at the junction of the browband and cheekpiece.

To avoid limiting the horse's breathing, the throatlatch needs to be the loosest attachment on the snaffle or any other bridle. You should be able to get a fist between the throatlatch and the horse's jaw.

Western Headstalls

The Western riding term for a bridle is a "headstall." There are several different types of western headstalls. Generally, they don't have as many pieces as the English bridle. Some headstalls have no noseband or browband, another one has no bit. There are, however, some extra pieces on some headstalls, including chains or straps that connect under the chin, that are not usually seen on other bridles.

Riding Vocab

The shanks of a headstall are metal pieces of various shapes which connect the mouthpiece to both the straps and chains of the headstall as well as the reins.

Some of the western headstalls look and are put on a horse quite differently from the snaffle bridle. A split-ear headstall has loops that fasten around the ears. The strap functions as both a browband and a cheekpiece, going around the horse's face on down to the bit.

Even more distinctive is the one-eared headstall, which fits and is secured at the top of the head over just one ear. Like a split-ear headstall, the strap goes around the sides of the horse's face and connects into the shanks.

There is also a futurity or futurity knot headstall, which includes a browband tied together in the middle with a fancy knot. This type of attachment is simply for ornamental purposes. It's used by people who want to make their horse stand out in a show or parade.

Equine Tip

Western bridles were designed to deal with the hot weather that many riders encounter and work in on desert trails. It's one of the many western riding traditions that came from the quite warm conditions encountered by Mexican riders called vaqueros.

The removal of some straps from the bridle, including the noseband and the browband, helps keep the horse cooler.

The Hackamore or Bosal

There is another western bridle that does not have any kind of bit. It is called a hackamore. Instead of restraining the horse with a bit, it pulls the horse back by the nose, poll, and chin. It's sometimes known as a bosal, which is the name for the lower part, or noseband, of a hackamore.

Riding Vocab

A fiador is a rope used in conjunction with a hackamore bridle. It's tied to the noseband and then circled around the horse's neck. When the reins pull on the headstall, the fiador keeps the noseband in place.

The mecate traditionally made of alternating white and dark horsehair but now more commonly made of artificial fibers, ties on the underside of the bosal to help hold it in place. The mecate, which is about 20 feet long, is then stretched out and turned into the reins. Usually, there is a popper, similar to the lash on a whip, which is attached to the end of the mecate.

If your horse's teeth or mouth are sensitive—remember a horse's teeth are always growing, and younger horses have new teeth coming in for several years—a hackamore is one alternative. Other western riders prefer it just because it is much easier to put on a horse than other bridles. You just pull the bosal up over the nose and lift the other strap, known as the hanger, up behind the ears. Then there are two other ropes used to hold it in place: the mecate, which also becomes the reins, and the fiador.

Riding with a Hackamore

Inexperienced riders should not use a hackamore since it requires a good deal of expertise not to pull the horse's head too hard. Though there is no bit in a hackamore, it can actually be more severe on a horse than the pressure of a bit.

The signals to the horse have to be short and quick when he's wearing a hackamore. Without a bit, you're not so much telling the horse to slow down as you are simply pulling his head back.

When riding with a bit-less bridle, you should ride with longer reins so you can make a loop with them, which gives you more pull if you need it. It also lets you open the reins wider to pull them in a bigger arc if desired.

The Curb Bit

As well as a hackamore, a western headstall usually works with a curb bit. While a snaffle bit only applies pressure to the corners of the mouth, a curb bit also applies pressure to the tongue and top of the mouth.

The piece outside the mouth that connects the mouthpiece of a curb bit to the cheekpieces and reins is called the shank. It is usually an angled piece of metal and functions the same way as the rings on a snaffle bit.

The mouthpiece on a curb bit has a port in its center. The more it is elevated, the more pressure is being applied.

The curb bit has a chain or strap that is tied under the horse's jaw and also applies restraint to the horse when the reins are pulled.

There are a number of optional pieces used in conjunction with a curb bit, such as the following:

➤ Lip strap: Keeps the curb chain in place and prevents the horse from grabbing hold of it with his mouth

➤ Bit hobble: Blocks the rings of the bit from being pulled into the mouth

➤ Shank hobble: Protects the shank from damage or intrusion

➤ Bit guard: Protects the bit from damage or intrusion

Kimberwick (Kimblewick in the UK) Bits

A Kimberwick is one of the mildest of the curb bits. It has D-ring attachments and shorter shank pieces, which minimizes the leverage. The amount of pressure of a Kimberwick bit varies depending on the way the rider is holding the reins.

Spade Bits

A spade bit is a more elaborate version of the curb bit, normally used only with highly trained horses. It is a traditional part of western riding, going back to the days of the vaqueros.

The shank pieces on the spade bit are usually ornamental. The mouthpiece contains extra parts, including a spoon, which is attached above the port.

Riding Vocab

When a combination bridle is in use, the snaffle bit is called the bradoon. It is attached by a bradoon hanger, which is also known more simply as a slip head.

Though the mouthpiece is bigger with more parts to it, the well-trained horse using the spade bit normally responds quickly to signals and feels less pressure from the extra pieces than horses being ridden with a regular curb bit.

Pelham Bit, Double Bridles, and Combination Bridles

These are all a combination of a curb and a snaffle bit. They have both the shank attachment of the curb and the ring attachment of the snaffle. When this type of bit is in use, the rider usually has to have reins in both hands. One rein is the curb bit, the other is the snaffle.

On a double bridle, also known as a weymouth, the snaffle bit is smaller than usual. It is behind the curb bit and more elevated.

Washing Your Bits

It's important to keep the bits clean. Horses do get a good deal of saliva on the bits, which can easily get on the corners of the mouthpiece and harden. It can corrode the parts and damage the fit. You should wash off the bits after every use.

CHAPTER 8

All About Saddles

In This Chapter

➤ Saddle parts

➤ English and western saddles

➤ How to put on a saddle

➤ Buying a saddle

In this chapter, you'll learn all you need to know about saddles. You'll learn the terms used for the various parts of a saddle and the differences between English and western saddles.

You'll learn about pads, a necessary piece of equipment for putting on a saddle, and you'll learn how to put on both a Western and an English saddle. Finally, you'll get information about the cost of buying a saddle and what to look for when buying a saddle.

Parts of a Saddle

Though there are many parts to a saddle, a lot of them aren't visible. That's because a saddle contains a great deal of padding and coverings, which allow it to stay together and operate smoothly.

The Tree

The tree is the name for the base of the saddle. All the padding and equipment is either attached right onto the tree or attached to the tree through another attachment. With all the padding and other parts placed on top of it, you can't actually see the tree unless you turn over the saddle.

The tree is traditionally made from wood—hence the name. The base of the tree is made up of two bars that run parallel along the length of the saddle. The bars bear the weight of the rider, so they need to be balanced properly and be the right size. If the bars are too big or too small, the saddle will not lay evenly on the horse's back, which will put too much pressure on the horse's spine.

The tree bars are traditionally made from high-quality wood cut to a specific pattern. The woods chosen are soft and flexible such as ash, cottonwood, or beech.

Once the saddle tree is carved into the proper shape, it's then sprayed with a substance, usually polyurethane, that will prepare it for the next step when a covering is placed over it, usually some kind of animal hide. Bull hide is considered the strongest and most durable hide. There are other coverings used that aren't as strong, including canvas or even cheesecloth.

Synthetic trees made of fiberglass and other materials are also available. Most of them are somewhat less reliable, but they are about half the price of trees made of wood.

Treeless Saddles

Treeless saddles are a recent development—sort of. In fact, the idea of a treeless saddle is to recreate the feeling of bareback riding, which is hardly new. Without a tree, the saddle has a much closer connection to the horse's movements. The horse, too, has a freer feeling of movement, especially through his shoulders. The treeless saddle is also lightweight, which is usually good for both horse and rider.

Horse Sense

Despite some advantages, treeless saddles are not universally loved. They seem to be the wrong choice for some activities, including jumping. If you're just starting to ride, you might want to wait a while before you try one.

The Top of the Saddle

The top of the saddle is made of various parts, including the pommel, the gullet, and the cantle.

➤ Pommel: The high front part of the saddle. It lifts up off the horse's neck so as not to rub on the horse's withers. On a western saddle, this area is also called the swell or the fork. It usually also contains a horn, which is not part of an English saddle.

➤ Gullet: The deep groove in the underside of the front of the saddle. The area between the two bars of the tree is known as the gullet channel.

➤ Cantle: The part at the back of the saddle seat that rises up. Proper riding form calls for the rider's backside to be against the cantle but not pressed back too hard onto it. The depth of the seat and cantle are more pronounced on western saddles, providing more support for the rider.

On a western saddle, the front part, with its horn and fork, is higher than the cantle in order to give the rider more leverage. On an English saddle, however, the saddle is lower at the pommel and higher toward the cantle. This makes it easier for the horse to move and especially for him to jump.

The padding for the seat and other areas of the saddle can be made of wool, fleece, or other comfortable and light materials. There are also saddles that use air as a type of cushion.

Stirrups

Stirrups are also known as irons, although they're not usually made of iron, but steel. On an English saddle, stirrups are pulled down from under the seat. On a western saddle, they are already attached and hanging down.

The open part of the stirrup, which holds the foot, is made up of two or three side pieces that are connected at the top with a bolted roller. The bottom of the stirrup, where the sole of the boot rests, is called the tread.

There are some other designs for stirrup seen around the world, including a boot stirrup, which is an actual shoe or slipper that you put your foot in rather than the circular opening of most stirrups.

Girths and Cinches

Girths are the straps that run under the horse's belly and connect the saddle from both sides. On a western saddle, the girth is called a cinch.

Girths and cinches are measured and sold by the inch. They are measured differently depending on which type of saddle you're using. On an English saddle, the girth is measured from buckle to buckle, with the buckles being up near the seat. The sizes go from 36 inches for a pony to 60 inches for a large horse.

The measurements for cinches on western saddles are several inches smaller than they are for English saddles. They are measured from the side of the saddle, rather than from near the seat. They range from 22 inches to 38 inches.

Girths and cinches come in several different materials, including fleece, nylon, and string, although the best quality ones are made of leather or mohair. The softer materials such as sheepskin or fleece are better if your horse is sensitive on his stomach or sides.

Breast Collars

On a western saddle, a breast collar is an attachment that goes around the chest of the horse and into the front of the saddle. It's used to hold and stabilize the saddle. Breast collars are also frequently used as ornamental pieces of equipment at western horse shows.

Side Reins, Martingales, and Tie Downs

Side reins, martingales, and tie downs are pieces of equipment that are used to get the horse's head into the proper position. Some of them are only used in training.

There are two kinds of martingales that are used by English riders:

1. Standing martingale: A strap attached to the horse's noseband and connected underneath the horse to the horse's girth. If the horse raises his head too far, the martingale will pull it down.

2. Running martingale: A strap that attaches to the girth, but then reaches up under the horse and attaches to the reins. If the horse lifts his head too high, the running martingale will apply leverage to the reins, which will then be felt in the bit.

Side reins are attachments that run from the girth on an English saddle to the bit. They work in a manner similar to a martingale but are used during training or lunging of the horse.

A tie down is what western riders use to prevent a horse from tossing his head too high. It's similar to a martingale but not as long. It's attached to the bridle from the cinch.

Saddle Sizes

Saddles are measured from the pommel to the cantle. On an English saddle, the sizes range from 15 inches for children to 18 inches for adults. The measurement for western saddles is done a little differently, and the sizes are a few inches smaller. A child's western saddle is about 12 inches; the standard adult sizes are 15 inches and 16 inches.

The saddle should not be putting weight on the horse's spine or pressing on his backbone. It should be forward of the horse's loins as well. If the saddle is putting pressure on those areas, it means the saddle is too big for the horse. The weight of the saddle should be on the lumbar muscles, which are on the side of the spine.

English Saddles

The English saddle evolved in the nineteenth century to replace the older, narrower saddle that was used for riding over longer distances, generally over flat grounds. The newer English saddles were created with both the pommel and the cantle lower and less cumbersome. This design made it easier to jump over any obstacles encountered.

Horse Sense

If your horse has a short back, the saddle also needs to be shorter. If the saddle is too long, it will be putting pressure on the horse's sides and also back by his loins and kidneys.

Eventually, English saddles were designed with lower stirrups for better use of the legs during riding.

English saddles are lightweight with as few parts as necessary. The idea is not to cut into the horse's freedom of movement as he runs, jumps, and goes over hilly terrain. That's why there is no horn on an English saddle, since that is put on the front of a western saddle to help the rider with his chores, not to help the horse.

Parts of an English Saddle

In addition to the lack of a horn and a lower pommel, the English saddles are distinguished from the western by their panels. The panels are the padding that provide a cushion between the horse and the saddle. There are front and rear panels on the saddle that are connected. The panels are traditionally made of wool, but are now also made of foam and sometimes are just air cushions.

Besides providing a cushion, the panels prevent the rider from making contact with the billet straps and buckle.

Billet straps are placed where the girth buckles attach. There are three billet straps under the flap. They hang down below the flap on dressage saddles, but they are shorter than the flaps on all-purpose or forward seat saddles.

Though there are three billet straps, only two are used. The third is a spare for safety reasons.

The flap is a wide pad that is under the seat of the English saddle and hangs down along the horse's sides to protect him from irritation caused by the rider's legs. The flap is designed with an adjustable length and width depending on the placement of the stirrups.

The English saddle also has a sweat flap, which is attached under the saddle flap. It is designed for draining the horse's perspiration off the bottom of the saddle.

English Stirrups

English stirrups are attached under the saddle to the stirrup bar, which is attached to the tree. The stirrup bar is connected to the stirrups through the stirrup leather, which required the creation of the stirrup leather keeper. The stirrup leather, which is about 1 inch wide, is pulled down to the desired length. The actual stirrup, with the opening for the foot, hangs below it.

The standard design of the English stirrup has two side bars that loop in an arc to create the opening for the rider's foot. There is an eye above the top of the stirrup through which the leather is attached. The tread at the bottom is straight, unpadded, and in either one or two pieces.

There are variations in English stirrups, including safety stirrups, which have elastic on the outside—the side away from the horse. These stirrups are used often by hunters and jumpers because they allow the rider to move more and adjust his legs.

The reason it's called a safety stirrup is because the elastic can detach in an emergency, such as when the rider is thrown from the horse but is still being dragged by the foot.

There are risks with a safety stirrup, since the weight is not distributed evenly and the elastic side is subject to extra wear. The band can break at any time, so it's important to keep checking the elastic to make sure it's still intact and safe.

Another stirrup designed to address riding dangers is the bent-leg stirrup. The outside piece is bent so that it is easy to remove the foot if the rider has been thrown. Since it's all metal, there is not as much risk of wear as there is with the safety stirrups.

English Saddles and Side Saddles

English saddles vary depending on the specific activity, such as showing, jumping, racing, or riding, of the English rider.

The side saddle is a unique type of English saddle that has been around for a long time. Originally, it was designed for women since it was considered inappropriate for them to sit astride a horse. Though it's still used by those who have problems sitting on top of a horse, its main use today is in shows and other special events.

A side saddle is constructed quite differently from most saddles. It has two pommels in the front, which provide extra control. Unlike other English saddles, the girths usually have three buckles and use all of the billet straps.

The rider in a side saddle remains balanced in the seat even though both legs sit on the left side of the horse. The seat in the saddle is wider to hold more of the thighs and buttocks.

A major difference of a side saddle as compared to other English saddles is in the stirrups. They are set much shorter than they are on most saddles, and they are attached further down. The flap is lower down on the left side, where the legs are. This keeps the rider's legs from hitting the horse's shoulder.

Western Saddles

Western-style riding is designed primarily for the activities of the rider. The horn in the front is used as a place to store the rider's rope, or to tie a rope that is connected to either another horse or another animal. The horn can also be used for leverage by the rider when he is mounting or dismounting the horse.

Western saddles are quite a bit heavier than English saddles. Their starting weight is about 30 pounds, about twice as much as an English saddle. But when all the usual gear is added, that weight can be doubled. However, even though the English saddle puts much less weight on a horse's back, the western saddle distributes the weight of the rider better because it is longer and wider.

Parts of the Western Saddle

Fenders is the western term for the flaps. Fenders are usually made of heavier leather and are thicker than flaps.

The area called the pommel on English saddles is also known as a swell and a fork in western saddles. It holds together the bars of the tree while also supporting the horn.

There are three kinds of swells on western saddles:

1. A fork, also known as the slick fork: Used by riders such as ropers who need to get out of the saddle quickly.

2. Swell fork: The most common, with a design that is more rounded than the A fork, which makes dismounting a little slower but safer.

3. Undercut swell: The rarest, with a different design that makes it easier for the rider to hang on when being bucked by an unruly horse.

Covering all this, for the comfort and safety of the rider, is the skirt, also known as the jockey. It is a piece of leather designed to prevent the rider from rubbing his leg on the stirrup bar.

Riding Vocab

A blevins buckle is perhaps the most popular type of stirrup buckle now used on western saddles. It contains pegs inside a sleeve. The leathers are then inserted and attached to the sleeve.

The features of the blevins buckle allow for quick adjustment, which is why it has becomes such a widely used piece of equipment.

Western Saddle Stirrups

Unlike English saddle stirrups, western stirrups are not detachable. The saddle leathers are connected right to the bar of the tree. Western stirrup leathers are also a good deal heavier and wider than the English stirrups. They're about 3 inches, or three times as wide as the English stirrup leathers. Western stirrups are usually set lower than English stirrups to allow for a straighter leg.

In the past, western stirrup leathers were adjusted to the proper length through strings, but that's now accomplished much more easily through the use of buckles.

Western stirrups also have a thicker and wider tread than you'll find on English stirrups. The wider tread is designed to deal with the higher and thicker heel of the western rider's boot. On western saddles, the tread has a covering called the tread wear leather that cushions the boot.

There are a number of varieties of western stirrups. The roper, the ox-bow, and the overshoe have variations in the shape of the side pieces. There is also a wide range of width among the treads from as narrow as 1 inch to as wide as 6 inches on a design known as the bell bottom. The width of the tread is determined by how much of the foot the rider wants to put in the stirrup.

An optional piece of equipment on western stirrups is a tapadero. It is a covering made of leather and is used on the side of the stirrups. The tapadero, sometimes just called taps, helps prevent the rider's foot from going all the way through the opening in the stirrup. It offers protection for the foot when the rider is going through brush or other sharp and potentially dangerous impediments. It can also provide some warmth when riding in the cold.

Saddle Strings and Dee Rings

Saddle strings are an attachment to a western saddle used to tie accessories, such as a lariat, a canteen, or a saddlebag.

Saddle strings are about ½ inch wide and are 2 to 3 feet long. They hang down in various locations on the saddle, depending on how many there are.

Usually, saddle strings are paired, with as many as eight on one saddle. If there are six strings, they hang from the front of the skirt and in the back under the cantle. If there are eight straps, there are two more below the fork.

Some western saddles do not have saddle strings but have Dee Rings (shaped like a D) that serve the same function. A dee-ring can also be used as an attachment for other pieces, including a breast collar.

Saddle Bags

A more convenient and modern way to carry your gear and belongings on a western saddle is in a saddle bag. Saddle bags come in whatever style you want and can be designed to carry almost anything. You can put a bottle in there, or a rope, wire cutters, pliers, etc. You can even get ones that will carry your gun.

It may not be like the old days of the west, but you can also get bags that are designed to carry your cell phone and possibly even your laptop.

Whatever you want to put in a saddle bag, it's usually attached to one of the saddle strings on the back of the saddle. There are also bags, like a cantle bag or a horn bag, designed to be carried in other locations.

Specialized Western Saddles

Western saddles are specialized for roping, cutting, barrel racing, and endurance, among other activities. All of these saddles are different and are designed for the specific needs of each of the various activities.

Riding Vocab

Some western riders refer to the pad as the blanket, which is not to be confused with the blanket used to cover and warm the horse. When the pad is called a blanket, it's usually thicker and heavier than normal, even for a western saddle.

Saddle Pads

Despite the name, the saddle pad is not designed for padding but to help keep the saddle clean. There is a saddle pad designed specifically for each type of saddle. Make sure your pad matches your saddle.

On English saddles, the pad needs to cover a wider area than the saddle, at least 1 inch wider on all sides. For western saddles, the pad is usually heavier and wider than the English saddle pad, reflecting the heavier weight of the western saddle. But the idea is the same.

A quite thin pad is desirable to help give you the feel of your horse's back. Generally, thick pads are more cumbersome, do not lay flat, and should be avoided.

Putting on the Pad

Before you put the pad on, it's a good idea to brush off the horse to take off any dirt that would otherwise be pinned under the saddle. Brushing the horse also helps keep the pad from getting dirty.

Also, check the pad before you put it on. Make sure it doesn't have any dirt on it, either, or a little stone or other debris that might annoy or bother the horse's skin.

Start by putting the pad near the withers on the horse's neck above where it will end up. Then slide it back toward his tail into the right place. By moving it back in this manner, you won't be making the horse uncomfortable by pushing the saddle against the horse's hair, which grows and is combed toward his tail.

Make sure you place the pad short of the horse's withers. Once you've gotten it into the right position, you're ready to put on the saddle.

Putting on an English Saddle

Just as you examined the pad, you should also check the bottom of the saddle. It might have something like a burr that could make the fit uneven and uncomfortable.

Many saddle pads, especially those used by English riders, have loops or buckles that connect the saddle to the pad. If your pad has such an attachment, begin by attaching the girth to the saddle through this opening.

On an English saddle, the girths are attached and buckled into the billet straps under the flap. Attach them first on the right side, then go around to the horse's left, pull the girth under the horse's belly, and attach the buckles to the corresponding billets on that side.

You don't want the saddle to be so tight that it hurts the horse, but it has to be on securely enough to stay in place. There should be just a slight bit of wiggle room for small adjustments.

Once the saddle is on, make sure it is on straight and that there are no tangled parts. Don't forget to check both sides.

Riding Vocab

An elastic girth has an elastic attachment on one end, which makes it easier to adjust the fit. If you have this kind of girth, the leather end is attached first, on the right side of the horse's saddle.

Putting on a Western Saddle

Since a western saddle can be fairly heavy, the best way to lift it on a horse's back is to get leverage from your legs. Be careful that the many hanging parts, from the stirrups to the fenders, do not bump the horse, especially by his head, which would be sure to spook all but the calmest of horses and make your day miserable. That's why you want to be swinging the saddle up somewhat toward the horse's tail, spinning it up and onto his back. As with an English saddle, make sure you do not have the saddle placed too far forward, as this could limit the movements of the horse's shoulders.

On a western saddle, instead of the billet straps, there is a leather piece called the latigo that comes attached to the side of the saddle. Unlike the billet straps, which are hidden under the flap, the latigo hangs down from the side of the saddle. It has both a strap and a loop to connect and secure the saddle into place.

Horse Sense

Don't try to be subtle when you're saddling your horse. If you're trying to put the saddle on so quietly that the horse won't know it, forget it. The horse should see the saddle and realize that you're putting it on him. Then he won't be startled when it gets put onto his back.

You should get him used to the little bumps and pulls during the saddling process. That way if something unexpected happens, like a gust of wind blows something out of your hand, he will be used to little things happening and won't get spooked.

The cinches on a western saddle attach on the right side of the saddle with a buckle. You pull the cinch underneath the belly to connect it with the latigo strap. Like a pulley, you keep stretching the latigo through its own loop and the loop on the cinch. Once you've adjusted the cinch to the correct length, you can wrap around any access part of the strap like you're tying a necktie to secure it in place.

Equine Tip

If you're out for a ride on a hot day and need a break, you can use your western saddle like a chair. After tying up the horse and taking off the saddle, you can set it down (carefully) on the ground and sit back in it. Just be careful you don't knock anything loose.

On some western saddles, there is a second cinch called the back cinch. There is usually no second latigo, so the second strap is designed to be buckled into the side of the saddle. The second cinch is used to keep the saddle secure during heavy-duty operations, such as when cattle or some other animal are tied to the horn.

Buying the Right Saddle

Other than a trailer, the saddle is likely to be the most expensive piece of equipment you will buy, which is why you want to get the right saddle for you and your horse. A decent new saddle will likely cost close to $1,000, though there are many that are much more expensive.

Your choice of saddle will depend on what kind of horse you have—not just his breed, but his size and the kind of riding you're going to be doing. If you're going to be jumping with your horse, you'll want the lighter-weight English saddle.

In a perfect world, every saddle will be available and you can get exactly the type of saddle you want, or think you want. In reality, you may only be able to shop at certain locations. Your choice might be limited, and that might also limit your activities. If you've got a good-sized hunter but the only saddle you can find that will fit him is a large western saddle, don't plan on doing any jumping with him, at least not with that kind of saddle.

If you're new to riding or have a new horse, you probably don't want to order a saddle through the mail or the Internet because you can't be sure of what you're doing. That is, unless you're getting advice from someone who does know what he's doing and what to shop for.

You can save money by buying a used saddle, and there are certain advantages to doing it. The leather should already be broken in and well treated. Used saddles are usually quite a bit cheaper than new ones, usually below $750.

You'll find that some used saddles for sale are actually quite old, having been in use for more than twenty or thirty years. But saddles have been compared to cars. In the same way that some classic cars and makes tend to keep their value as long as they're given proper care, so too can a well-kept older saddle continue to be priced at the high end of the market.

But be careful. Buying a used saddle can be a risk the same way that buying a used helmet can be. There could be wear in places where you wouldn't know to look, and this could result in some real risk. Unless you're an expert, don't buy an old saddle before getting someone who's very knowledgeable to okay it. The extra savings won't be worth it if you take a bad fall.

Additional Costs

Keep in mind the other expenses for the parts you're adding to the saddle. If you're using a breastplate, for instance, that will cost you somewhere between $100 and $200. A martingale will run you anywhere from $50 to $125. If you want a saddlebag, that will cost you between $50 and $100. Girths or cinches usually cost under $50. A saddle pad costs around $200.

All these pieces can have expenses added either with fancy designs or extra optional attachments.

If you've got a lot of money to put into your riding experience, you can also buy a saddle stand, where you can keep your saddle. The cost of a stand is near $1,000, pretty close to the cost of the saddle itself.

CHAPTER 9

Your Riding Gear

In This Chapter

➤ Wearing the right clothes

➤ Selecting helmets and boots

➤ All about whips

In this chapter, you'll learn about the clothes and boots you'll be wearing and the equipment you will be using when you ride a horse. You'll learn about helmets and the important safety requirements they must meet.

You'll also learn about the only piece of equipment you'll be carrying with you when you get on a horse, your whip.

Getting Dressed

If you get to such an advanced state of riding that you're competing in horse and rider competition, you know the clothing you'll be wearing. Either you'll have a fancy coat and white pants for dressage or cross-country riding, or neat western apparel for western competition. But even if you never get to that level in your riding, you still need to dress properly for your ride. That means your clothes need to be safe. You don't want your clothes flapping around or in danger of being caught on anything, which could harm you and your horse.

Equine Tip

If you're riding in cold weather, remember that clothing can't be so heavy that it will weigh you down and cause you to lose your balance.

If it's hot and there is the possibility you'll be sweating quite a bit, you'll want to wear clothing that can absorb the moisture. Though your tack should be mostly water-resistant, perspiration is still a concern. You'll need to make sure you're using reins that won't get slippery and become difficult to grip. You might also consider lightweight gloves.

If your reins are made of leather and not some synthetic material, they can get warped in the rain, so they need to be hung up and stretched after they've gotten wet.

Shirts

Your shirt should be tucked in when you're riding. That might look bad, but it could become a safety hazard if the wind blows it about.

A good tip is to wear a shirt with a stiff collar. Never mind whether this is appealing fashion for you—the stiff collar will let you feel if you're keeping your back straight and your shoulders positioned in the right direction. If you have somebody watching, helping, or training you, the stiff collar will help him see if your position is correct.

Pants

Western riders usually wear jeans, though they often find them too constricting when mounting a horse. The advantage of jeans is that they are made of strong denim, a material designed to withstand the rugged wear they'll get during a ride.

Many who ride English-style wear jodhpurs. They are pants that go all the way down the leg to the ankle. They are usually worn outside the boots. Sometimes a clip is used to keep the jodhpurs attached to the boots.

Jodhpurs are made of material that stretches easily. The inner leg, the part that makes contact with the horse, is made of a different material that is stronger.

Riding breeches are shorter than jodhpurs and are designed to fit inside the boot. The knees are not reinforced on breeches as they are on jodhpurs, unless they are what are known as reinforced breeches.

Helmets

You'll want to make sure that the helmet you purchase has been approved for use. There are organizations that certify riding helmets for safety. You'll want to make sure that the helmet you purchase has their stamp of approval. Even though bicycle or skateboarding helmets may save you money, they aren't tested for the type of impact you could have falling off a horse.

Riding Vocab

In the United States, helmets should be certified either by the American Society of Testing Materials (ASTM) or the Safety Equipment Institute (SEI).

Naturally, you want to get a helmet that fits you. That means that when it's on your head, there should be no wiggle room. A good way to make sure the helmet is on correctly is to bend your head down before you attach the strap. If the helmet is the right size, it should stay in place without the extra bit of securing that comes from the strap.

The sliders are the part of the helmet that have the strap and buckle. The sliders should be near the ear, not hanging by the chin. If they are too low, the helmet will become turned when you fasten the strap.

Since your safety is the most important factor, you shouldn't buy a used helmet unless it's been recertified by someone who knows what they're looking for. You probably won't know what problems an old helmet may have.

You'll want to get a helmet that is adjustable to make sure that it fits properly. You'll also want one with a strap that will make your helmet secure as well as comfortable when it is fastened around your chin. The interior shell should be removable so it can be cleaned.

The best helmets have ventilation ports to increase circulation. Keeping yourself cool is not just about comfort, but a safety precaution as well. By keeping yourself from getting too hot, especially around your head, you'll help keep yourself mentally sharp, an important part of safe riding.

Equine Tip

If you live in a warm climate, you would do well to invest in a helmet with extra ventilation. It will help prevent you from overheating and let you ride longer with more pleasure.

When you do attach the strap, it should be tight, but not uncomfortably so. There should be enough room to get a finger between the strap and your chin. Make sure the helmet does not settle down below your eyebrows.

Equine Tip

Wearing goggles is a good idea, especially if you're going to be riding in the rain or in very dusty conditions, since you don't want to get water or dirt in your eyes while you're riding.

If you're wearing goggles, you'll want to bring several pairs so you can take off the ones that get too wet or covered with dirt. Experienced riders wear several pairs of goggles on top of each other. When one pair gets too wet or dusty, they simply pull it down around their neck and the next pair is already in place.

Boots

The type of boots you get depends on what kind of riding you're going to do. Most English-style riders wear tightly fitting high boots that either reach up to their knees or gets very close. Boots used for western-style riding are usually not as high, only going to about mid-calf.

Most casual riders wear shorter boots that are tightened with a zipper in the back. This provides for more comfort and also helps keep the foot stable during riding.

The most important advice for wearing boots is to wear a solid, fairly high heel. Western boots are noted for this trait. A high heel helps prevent the foot from sliding out of the stirrup. Leather boots are the best quality, though rubber boots are also effective. They are also versatile and can be used for other activities around the barn besides riding.

Remember that all your leather goods, including all the parts of your tack, need to be cleaned and oiled regularly to keep them in proper condition.

Horse Sense

Spurs are an optional piece of equipment that you shouldn't need or want. The spurs in use now are not as sharp or dangerous as the ones some riders used in the past. The modern ones are blunt and made of rounded metal. Inexperienced riders should not be using even these mild spurs, which are designed to ask the horse for more speed or elevation for a jump.

After some training, a horse will respond just fine if you press your boot against his side to signal him. There's no need to increase his fears or raise his anger by jabbing his side with anything sharper.

The Whip

One other item you'll need for your ride is a whip. It is the one piece of riding equipment that is neither attached to the horse nor worn by you.

Horse whips come in a wide variety of sizes and makes. The basic designs are the same, with a handle at the end, a shaft of varying flexibility, and the end piece, usually designed to make contact with the horse, known as the lash, or the popper.

This may all sound primitive, but you're not going to use your whip to beat or punish your horse. You carry it strictly as a way of encouraging or signaling him. In most cases, the whip is just a way of reinforcing what you want the horse to do if he hasn't gotten the message from either your verbal or physical signals.

Horse Sense

You should practice with your whip before you use it. This is especially true if you're using a long whip for lunging or training (see "Lunging Whip" below). If you don't know what you're doing and you end up hitting the horse where or when you don't want to, then he'll become afraid of the whip and you won't be able to use it effectively. He should respect the whip and understand that you're using it to give him direction.

Remember to show your horse a lot of love when he gives a proper response to your use of the whip. That means to pet him on the neck and praise him in a kind and friendly way.

Dressage Whip

There are several kinds of whips used for riding, the longest of which is a dressage whip. It's normally 3 to 3½ feet long. It begins with a narrow tip and proceeds with a long, thin shaft.

The reason that the dressage whip is that long is because it's designed to allow the rider to maintain his seat while being able to reach around and tap the hindquarters.

Riding Crop

Also known as a bat, the riding crop is shorter than other whips, about 2 to 3 feet long. It's found in many sports involving horses, including rodeos, show jumping, hunt competitions, and racing. To use it, the rider holds the reins in one hand while tapping the horse behind him on the side. It's designed to encourage the horse to increase his speed or to lift for a jump.

Show Cane

This whip is now rarely seen except at certain horse events. It has much less flexibility than other horse whips and is more for appearance than use. Normally, it's made of high-quality wood and polished to provide a fancy appearance.

Hunting Whip

A hunting whip is 2 to 3 feet long with a long lash. It does not make contact with the horse but is used primarily during fox hunts to ward off the hounds if they get too close to the horse.

The shaft of the hunting whip, also called the stock, is stiff, made of cane or other hard materials. It's often covered in leather to make gripping easier in wet conditions.

The hunting whip also has a hook on the end designed specifically for opening gates as the riders move around estates and the countryside. There is usually a long leather piece called a thong attached to the end. It's the primary piece used to move away the dogs. If a hunting whip doesn't have a thong, it's known as a hunting crop.

Quirt

A quirt is a shorter whip, primarily used in western riding activities. It is used more as a noisemaker. It is made of braided leather and makes a loud snap when it hits the horse or, more often, some other object. Its main use now is to signal, or really frighten, cattle to move on.

Lunging Whip

When you're lunging, or working out your horse, you're usually about 20 feet away from him. That's why this whip is much longer than the whips used for riding. The shaft of the lunge whip is usually at least 4 feet long with a lash about the same length.

Again, this whip is not designed for hurting, punishing, or threatening the horse, but to signal him to change directions or to pick up the pace.

Driving Whips

The driving whip was much more common in the days of stagecoach travel. They are used to encourage and direct horses pulling carriages or carts.

The shaft of the driving whip is about the same length as a lunging whip—4 feet—but has a shorter lash, only about 1 foot long.

Very similar but even rarer now are the buggy whip, which has a short lash, and the coach whip, which has a longer lash.

Other Whips

There are other designs of whips within the various types. Children's whips, naturally, are much shorter. There are also whips, mostly antiques, designed strictly for use by women. They were not only a bit smaller than those designed for men, but were also usually in brighter, more "feminine" colors.

There are also older whips made of material no longer used for various reasons, mostly because of taste. They were made of elephant skin and tusks, or crocodile skin.

Equine Tip

On warm days when a horse is sweating a great deal, riders often use their whip to scrape the sweat off their horse's body. It can keep the reins, among other items, from getting wet, and it can also make the horse more comfortable. Of course, wait until your horse is stopped before you try to do this.

PART THREE

Riding

 Preparing Yourself to Ride

---

In This Chapter

➤ Getting yourself prepared

➤ Stretching your body

➤ Mental preparation

In this chapter, you'll learn the best way to get your body ready for your ride. These preparations will minimize your risk of injury and will also develop your body so you can improve your riding skills.

Don't forget that you need to be mentally sharp for your journey, so you'll also learn how to get your mind focused and your thoughts in order.

Warming Up

Whatever type of exercise program you are already using can be adapted as a fitness regimen for riding. It doesn't matter if you like Pilates, yoga, or some other program. The fundamentals of exercise and stretching can be used to improve riding performance.

You can tailor your routine for the specific demands placed on your body by riding. Although your whole body needs to be flexible, you need to pay special attention to certain parts that get more of the pressure and vibration when you're on your horse.

Raising Your Body Temperature

You want to raise your body temperature before you stretch, so a little aerobic exercise is a good way to start. You could begin with a little jogging in place, preferably on your toes, which will help warm up your ankles. You'll then want to bounce a little on your feet and then lift your knees while you're running in place to help stretch out those joints and the surrounding tendons.

If you have a physical condition that makes any of these warm-ups difficult, it's fine to do something else. The main idea during this preliminary part of your routine is just to get your heart beating faster, which will make the rest of your program easier.

Equine Tip

The goal of exercising is to (safely!) increase your body temperature because that's what helps make your body more flexible and better able to respond to your horse's movements. But the time you spend preparing yourself to ride will vary according to the weather. You'll need more time to warm up if it's cold. The body won't loosen up as quickly in lower temperatures, so you'll need to extend your exercise time to get your heart beat up. Warmer weather, naturally, has the opposite effect, raising your body temperature more quickly.

Stretching to Promote Flexibility

Though your horse may weigh more than half a ton, the proper fitness program for a rider does not emphasize power. You don't need to lift huge loads in the weight room. In order to get what you want, which is a feeling of harmony with your horse, you need to train your body to be coordinated. In the process, you'll want to improve your strength in ways that will specifically help you in the saddle.

A long time spent riding your horse will place a good deal of pressure on your neck, shoulders, and back. You'll want to get these areas stretched and loosened before you get on your horse. This also means massaging certain bones and joints to relieve tension that may have built up.

Your goal is to improve the mobility of your spine, which in turn will make you more coordinated. Your movement in the saddle will then flow more readily and effectively.

The Neck

Naturally, riding your horse requires keeping your head upright. That's not just to make sure that you two are going in the right direction and that there's nothing dangerous in your path. As you'll discover when you learn about the proper seat in the saddle, keeping your head upright is also the way to stay balanced and in control of your horse. But keeping your neck straight for long periods can cause a good deal of stiffness and tension. Stretching and messaging this area before you ride is a good way to limit any possible discomfort and keep you riding safely.

It's always a good idea to be careful when stretching any area of the body, but, of course, safety is particularly important when stretching the neck. Take everything slow, and certainly stop if you're feeling pressure.

To begin with, gently turn your head from side to side. Slowly bend your head forward and backward, and then in a circular motion. These moves should get your neck feeling loose and stretched.

Top of the Spine, Back of the Head

There is a vital spot at the top of the neck known as the atlanto-occipital joint. This is where your skull connects to the first vertebrae.

Since the atlanto-occipital joint is connected to the spine, it affects a lot more than just your neck. If you can increase the flexibility in this joint, it will also benefit you all the way down to the base of the spine, where you're sitting on the horse.

Once you've located this joint, spend about a minute massaging the area with the fingers of both hands before you begin your ride. This will help minimize any tension that may have built up in that region.

Since the skull also can develop a good deal of tension, it's a good idea to spend some time massaging the back of your head. Just be careful not to rub too hard and give yourself a headache.

The Shoulders, Chest, and Rib Cage

The impact of riding your horse should be spread evenly from your head to your seat, but when the area around the center of your spine is stiff, the vibrations will be absorbed by your chest and rib cage. The result is that you will not shift and move in rhythm with the horse. This will also result in an uncomfortable or downright painful feeling through the ribs and chest.

Stretching this area of the body is a fairly simple activity. While standing, stretch both your arms out wide and rotate them in a circular motion, first forward, then backward. After a while, increase the arc of the circles and increase the speed of your movements. This will give your shoulders, chest, and rib cage a good stretch.

The Hips, Sacroiliac, and Pelvis

Sitting in any location for a good while can put strain on your lower back, buttocks, and pelvis, but being in the saddle for an extended period can really cause a good deal of stiffness. It's important to gently stretch this region before you start riding.

Riding Vocab

The term seat bones used in riding is not a phrase you'll find in any medical book. It's the riding term for the part of your body that presses down in the saddle. Since it's not an actual part of the body, the location of the bones can vary depending on who is describing them. Some expert riders say the seat bones are at the bottom of the pelvis, but others list them as being at the top of the thighs.

If you want to know for sure where your seat bones are, just check what bones are pressing down in the saddle once you've mounted your horse.

While standing, put your hands on your hips and start bending from side to side. The next move is to finish your stretch by extending first one arm down your leg, then the other. Then stretch each arm separately over your head.

After you've finished these stretches with your arms, return them to your hips, then swing around in a circular motion, first in one direction, then in the other.

The Legs

There are unusual pressures put on your legs while riding your horse. Keeping them wrapped around the horse and clutching them to his side can cause a good deal of strain and tension to develop.

There are many good exercises for stretching the legs. Riders specifically should concentrate on keeping the thighs stretched, because that is an area that gets particular pressure when you're in the saddle.

One approach is to sit down on the floor with your legs spread. Reach toward your toes, first over one leg, then over the other. If you're flexible enough, you can put your head down between your legs, which will further stretch the inner thighs.

If you're new to leg stretches, do them slowly. As you continue to perform these stretches, your legs will get more and more limber, and the stretching will go from a somewhat uncomfortable feeling to the good feeling of being limber.

If, for whatever reason, you're uncomfortable getting down on the floor to stretch, you can accomplish much of the same standing up. Turn to the left and bend your left leg while keeping your right leg straight. Lower the upper part of your body and hold the stretch for ten seconds (if you can). Then repeat the stretching in the other direction.

When You're Not Riding

On days when you are not getting on your horse, it's still important to work out. If you're only riding one or two days a week, you can't ignore your fitness the rest of the time and expect to make up for it in the minutes before you get in the saddle.

On at least a couple of the days when you're not riding, you'll want to do some kind of aerobic exercise. Whether it's walking, running, playing tennis, or something else, anything that gets your heart rate elevated will, of course, help your overall fitness, but will also keep you fit for riding.

If at all possible, keep stretching your body the way you would on riding days. The exercises don't need to be as long or as concentrated, but you want to keep yourself limber and flexible.

You may also want to do some strength training on the days when you're not riding. You can get some fairly light barbells to do curls and other exercises that will help keep your arms, shoulders, and hands strong. About five to ten minutes of careful, concentrated lifts should suffice.

Make sure you're using a weight you can handle comfortably. Also, remember not to put too much pressure on your elbows when you're using weights.

Mental Focus

Sometimes you may not be ready to ride. Your concentration may not be there or other thoughts are distracting you. But you need to get ready. If your body is slumped over, you need to straighten up. Good posture will help you get focused and make it easier for you to feel assertive.

A major part of sports psychology is visualization. Athletes in all sports have been instructed to go through this procedure before their actual competition. You may have seen Olympic skiers mentally rehearsing their trip before they head down the mountain. They do this so they are well prepared for their journey.

Riders can and should do the same thing. Rehearse in your head where you'll go and what you might encounter on your trip. This is really a good idea if you've reached the level of riding where you're competing in shows, cross-country races, or jumping competitions. But even if you're just out for a nice ride with your horse, you'll want to prepare mentally.

Of course, you may be riding your horse just because it's a fun and pleasurable experience. But you can't forget that there are also dangers. Most of the problems encountered by riders on their journeys are caused by a lack of mental focus. Letting your mind wander while you're riding can lead to falls and other accidents.

Horse Sense

A main reason that a lack of concentration is dangerous for a rider is that the horse can lose his focus as well. When a horse becomes relaxed while moving comfortably on a trail, something like a loud noise or the sudden flight of a bird can jar him more than usual.

If you've also let your concentration slip during the ride and don't have full control, the sudden moves of the horse can have disastrous results such as the horse crashing into a tree or simply tossing you from his back.

You already know that practicing the many stretches of yoga is a good way to get yourself ready to ride. The fundamentals of mental preparation taught by yoga are also useful for riding your horse. They will get you focused and help you clear your mind before your ride.

CHAPTER 11

Getting Your Horse Ready

In This Chapter

➤ Leaving the barn safely

➤ Preparing your horse

➤ Getting on board

➤ After the ride

In this chapter, you'll learn the proper way to get your horse out of his stall and prepared to be active. You'll find out how to get your horse stretched, focused, and happy before you ride him.

Before you can experience the joy of your journey, you'll need to know the proper and safe way to get on your horse's back. In this chapter, you'll learn how to get onto a horse as well as how to take care of him and his equipment after you finish your ride.

Leading a Horse

Walking your horse sounds like something that should be easy—just attach a rope to his bridle and lead him away. But your horse may not go along with the plan. He could be stubborn, he could be unhappy, or his instincts could cause him to object to the way you're handling him.

When walking, or leading, your horse out of the barn, you need to let the horse know that you're in control. When you slow down or stop, the horse should do the same. If he gets ahead of you, he is not following your commands. As is often the case with horses, repetition is the best training. You need to take the horse back and keep walking him until he finally gets the idea that you are the leader and that when you stop, he should stop, too.

Even if you're leading a disciplined and cooperative horse that follows your commands, there are still a few dangers that need to be avoided. Never forget that your horse is much stronger than you are. Since he is also a flight animal, always ready to bolt when he feels threatened, you need to have him under control at all times.

You must keep a firm grip on the rope because you do not want it to get wrapped around your hand. That could lead to a potentially dangerous situation in which the horse might suddenly be dragging you along the ground.

 You also need to stay a few feet to the side of him while leading. If you're too close to him and something frightens him, you won't have time to react, and in his panic he might run you over. If he starts to buck or pull, the only way you can control him is if you have several feet of the rope's slack in your hand, which gives you much more leverage.

Horse Sense

It's a good idea to look straight ahead while leading your horse, and not just so you don't veer off into a fence or a tree. If you're looking around while the two of you are walking together, the horse might wonder what you're looking at and stop. He might also lose confidence in your direction. But if you are looking forward and leading with a confident stride, the horse is likely to stay focused, and your task is made easier.

The Rope

There are a lot of lead ropes to choose from. Cotton, polyester, nylon, even chain ropes are available and used widely. The most common lengths of rope used for leading a horse are 12 and 14 feet. If you have a bigger horse, you'll want the longer rope, which will not only allow him more room to move but can give you more control. For you and your horse's safety, you need a rope that is strong enough not to tear or get tangled. You also want it to last a while and not be subject to abrasion.

Equine Tip

Your choice of lead rope will depend partly on your environment. If you're around harsh weather in an area with difficult or slippery terrain, you'll need a stronger, and probably more expensive, rope than you would if you lived in a mild climate with level ground.

Lunging Your Horse

The standard way to exercise a horse before he is ridden is known as lunging, sometimes spelled longeing. In Western riding, it is known as loping.

In lunging, a rope called a lunge line is attached to the horse. Some riders use the lead rope as the lunge line, but normally a different, longer rope is used. The lunge line is normally between 15 and 20 feet long, though some trainers who use lunge ropes up to 40 feet long.

The rope you choose needs to be both strong enough to control the horse and sturdy enough so it won't blow about on a windy day.

Equine Tip

A horse feels constricted when he is in his stall most of the day. So lunging your horse first thing will make him quite cooperative. If you let the horse run around a paddock or other area while attached to the lunge line, the horse will enjoy the freedom of being outside and will be grateful and cooperative for the rest of the lunging.

After you lunge him that way a few times, he'll be a happier horse because he will know you'll let him play when you start.

When a horse is being lunged, he is brought into an open area, where he responds to the commands of the rider or trainer. Occasionally, a whip is used for direction. Normally, the horse is walked in a circle, slowly at first, with the trainer or rider gradually extending the rope to give the horse a larger arc to follow. The horse then goes through his various strides, including the walk, the canter, and the trot. The goal is to get the horse into a good rhythm with good balance.

A cavesson is used for lunging and fits snugly across the horse's face below the noseband with the top part secured behind the ears. It is placed over the bridle and fitted securely, more tightly than the attachments of the bridle. The cavesson has a latch in the middle where the lunge line is hooked.

One way some riders use lunging is to get the horse tired before the ride, to take away his excess energy, which would likely make him uncooperative on the trail. This is known as getting the buck out of the horse. Riders or trainers sometimes take up to an hour for this purpose, about twice as long as the normal time needed for lunging.

If a horse hasn't been out of the barn for a few days, lunging is used to stretch his muscles and to once again get him comfortable taking commands. It's also a good way to get the attention of a horse that may be too relaxed or even lazy.

Another purpose of lunging is to calm down a horse that may become tense or nervous after being saddled for the first time in a while. Lunging gives him a chance to once again get used to moving around with the equipment.

If you lunge your horse every day, it's a good idea to vary his routine. If you follow the same steps and preparations every time, it won't be long before he becomes resentful and uncooperative at what he feels is endless and uninteresting repetition.

As the horse gets more training and becomes more cooperative, less time will be needed for lunging. A well-trained horse may not need any lunging at all, as long as he has been ridden enough recently so that he is properly stretched and alert for the ride.

Equine Tip

On days when weather conditions may be too severe to go out or if trails are snowed in or too slippery, riders will clear a small area so they can at least lunge their horses. It's the best way to keep a horse both focused and limber.

Keeping Your Horse Calm

By their nature, horses are cautious and often jittery. Do not let your actions give your horse any reason to become more nervous. In order to keep your horse calm, you need to be calm yourself. A horse will usually reflect your mood. If you are bringing outside tensions to the barn, the horse will sense it and will resist it. Do not let your actions give your horse any reason to become more nervous.

Your posture has an effect on the calmness of the horse. You need to stand relaxed and avoid making sudden movements that might frighten him. He might also be bothered by your voice if he thinks you are talking too loud or if he thinks you're agitated.

Equine Tip

Looking a horse in the eye can be a problem. Just a casual look might be fine, but the horse is likely to be bothered by a long stare right at his face. His survival instincts usually take such a look as a threatening act.

Horses also don't like you walking straight at them. The better idea is to angle your shoulder slightly when you're walking in their direction. A horse finds this approach less threatening.

Certain breeds of horses are more high-strung than others. Older horses are usually calmer than younger ones, and geldings are normally much calmer than stud horses. All of these facts should have been taken into consideration when you selected a horse to own or ride.

The Nervous or Tense Horse

Be aware of the signals that your horse is giving you. He'll let you know if something is bothering him. If you ignore your horse's signs that he is tense, his anger and frustration might grow to the point where he is uncontrollable.

An anxious or nervous horse moves around more than normal. One sure sign that a horse is anxious is if he is tossing his head a good deal. Another sign is if his ears are up. Something is making him uncomfortable and his ears indicate he is not relaxed but on heightened alert.

An even more serious and dangerous situation would be if your horse becomes so agitated that he doesn't want to move at all. Not only does he refuse to go when you ask him to, he fights you hard, bucking and rearing.

If your horse is exhibiting these problems, you need to find out what's bothering him. This could be tough and may require some detective work to determine if there is a problem in or around his stall. It's also possible his equipment is not on him properly and may be hurting him. His saddle might be too tight, or the bit and reins may be uncomfortable.

Even if you find the problem, you will still need to make sure that your horse is calm before you try to ride him. If he trusts you from your time together, you can show him that you're still his friend. Rub him gently and assuredly on the neck. Rub his nose, rub his back, and offer him some treats as well. This will relax him and let him know you will protect him.

Mounting Your Horse

Traditionally, horses are led and mounted from the left side. There are guides to riding from more than 2,000 years ago that refer to the left side as the near side of the horse, and the right side as the far side. There is an unconfirmed legend that this tradition started because soldiers always carried their weapons on their left side and it was much safer to mount their horses from the left. This legend goes back to the time before stirrups were invented and riders were taking a flying leap to get on their horses.

Your horse should not be mounted until you get him into an open area. It's too dangerous to try to get on a horse when you're close to a doorway or you're in an area with a low roof. But even if you have reached an apparently safe location, it's still a good idea to make sure there is nothing around that will scare the horse, endangering him and you. Look out for birds, a tractor about to start, or other horses soon to be coming through.

Final Checklist

Once you're confident that the horse will not be distracted, the first step is to make sure that he's standing properly. This means he is neither bunched up nor stretched out. A horse that is bunched up is standing with his legs too close together; one that is stretched out are standing with legs legs that are too far apart. If the horse's legs are not in the proper position, he will not be able to take your weight, at least not comfortably.

The next thing to do is check the saddle to make sure it's cinched properly. You certainly don't want it to slip or twist. Next, adjust the stirrups to the proper length, pulling them out from the side of the saddle. This is known as running the irons down. Finally, you're ready to get on your horse.

Getting on a Horse

When the horse is ready, your first step is to take the reins with your right hand. Then you should put your left hand about halfway up the horse's neck, above the withers. After you make sure the left stirrup is turned to face you, put your left foot all the way into this stirrup. The foot should be pointing down.

At this point you might want to just grab the horse's mane, put your right hand on his hindquarters, and pull yourself up by your hands. Don't do it; it will cause your horse to lose his balance or start moving.

The proper next step is to start hopping or bouncing on your right foot. You're doing this to get a rhythm before you straighten your left leg until your right heel is level with the left one that is already in the stirrup.

Horse Sense

Once you're elevated, a technique used by some riders is to reach over and pat the right side of the horse to get the horse ready for your arrival on that side. If you don't do this, it's possible that it might surprise and upset the horse when your leg swings over. Just because the horse feels your presence on his left side does not mean he's expecting you to come over to his other side.

You're now elevated, with your left foot in the stirrup and your right foot at the same level. The next step is to move your right hand to the pommel on an English saddle or the horn on a western saddle. Use this hand to help lift you as you swing your right leg up and over to the other side of the horse. Be careful not to kick the horse or the saddle while you're getting on.

When you're finally up on the horse, with your right leg over the side, do not just drop down heavily into the saddle, as this will jar the horse. Settle down gracefully and gently—or at least as gracefully and gently as you can—into the saddle. Then get your right foot secured in the stirrup.

Other Ways to Mount

If you're not tall enough to get up onto a horse's back, do not be afraid to get help. A mounting block is the equivalent of a short ladder, usually consisting of three steps. The mounting block is a sturdy piece of equipment, unlike a chair or stool, created to help shorter people mount horses.

The technique for mounting from the block is the same as from the ground, with the rider putting the left foot in the stirrup and bouncing with the right foot before getting on board.

Some riders like to use a mounting block even if they are tall enough because they feel the added height allows them to get into the saddle while putting less pressure on the horse's back.

If you have trouble getting on your horse by yourself, getting a boost from another person is another solution. In horse racing, jockeys, who are generally quite short, are usually given a leg up. The jockey places his left foot in a helper's hands and is boosted up so he can get onto the saddle. He then secures both feet into the stirrups.

In Sync

There are different theories about how to deal with a horse that starts moving as soon as you get on board. The most common approach is to pull the horse backward and return to where you started. The rider might even dismount and start all over if that's what it takes to let the horse know he is not to move until you are ready. Eventually, the horse should get the notion to wait until signaled to go.

If your horse is uncooperative and insists on starting to move each time you get on him, another approach is to hold the reins tight and keep him standing still after mounting. You can do this for a while, maybe half a minute. This will teach the horse that he's supposed to wait until you signal him before he leaves.

Cooling Down

After you finish your ride, you can't just put a horse back in his stall. He needs to be cooled down. Once you get all the gear off him and put his halter on him, he needs to be washed off, either with a sponge or a low-pressure hose. If it's a really warm day, this should be done immediately.

The horse is then walked about for a while. Horses can quickly get cold when they're wet, so unless it's really warm, you will need to wrap your horse in a blanket or sheet designed to prevent his temperature from dropping too much.

At a large stable, the person who walks the horse after a ride is fittingly called the "hot

Riding Vocab

Walking a horse after a workout to cool him down is called the hot walk, not because the ground is hot, but because the horse is. At a large stable, the person who walks the horse after a ride is fittingly called the hot walker. Some facilities have mechanical hot walkers, which have a lead rope that attaches to the horse's halter. The horse is then "lead" around slowly. The automatic hot walker is a little reminiscent of a carousel.

walker." At some facilities, there are mechanical hot walkers, which have a lead rope that attaches to the horse's halter. The horse is then led around slowly. The automatic hot walker is a little reminiscent of a carousel.

After getting his hot walk and bath, the horse is then returned to his stall, probably anxious to get his feed. Don't forget to take care of all the equipment, cleaning everything and hanging everything back in the appropriate place in the tack room.

CHAPTER 12

Riding Your Horse

In This Chapter

- ➤ Getting you and your horse balanced
- ➤ Proper use of the equipment
- ➤ Differences between English and western riding
- ➤ Avoiding danger

In this chapter, you'll learn the importance of the connection between you and your horse. When the two of you are out on your journey, it's possible to reach a level of cohesion where your horse seems to be anticipating your thoughts and you have a sense of where he is going even before he moves.

There are, however, some important actions you need to take before the two of you can attain such a high level of teamwork. You simply can't be in harmony with your horse if you are sitting improperly in the saddle, using the equipment incorrectly, or not paying attention to the signals the horse is giving you.

Even if everything seems to be going smoothly on your ride, it can all still be ruined if you start making wrong or dangerous moves. In this chapter, you'll learn what dangers to avoid and what precautions to take.

Being in Harmony

Once you're ready to head out to the trail, or wherever you two are heading, all the work you have put in with the horse should be rewarded. If your time spent with the horse preparing him for your ride has made him feel happy, confident, and comfortable, he'll carry that away from the barn and out on your journey. If your horse feels you're his friend, he'll want to please you and follow your directions.

But all that good work you put in to gain your horse's respect and trust can be quickly undone. When you are out on the trail, a feeling of harmony between you and your horse is only possible if both of you are properly balanced. No matter how much good preparation you've put in, none of it will be of much use on your ride unless the two of you have assumed the proper positions.

The horse will need to adjust his natural balance when you get on board. He will feel the extra weight on the front of his body, known as the forehand. Before the horse starts to move, you need to make sure that he has adjusted the position of his hind legs so that they are further underneath his body. If the horse doesn't make this adjustment, his hind legs will be pushing you forward rather than supporting you, and he won't become balanced or be able to move comfortably.

The Proper Seat

Your seat is the key to your balance, and the key to a proper seat is the placement of your seat bones. Once you are mounted, your seat bones need to be set deep in the lowest part of the saddle.

If you're in the saddle correctly, you will achieve an independent seat, which means your position has made you secure on the horse without the use of any other part of your body. Your legs on down to your feet should feel comfortable against the horse's side. You should feel in control.

When you are well balanced, you will be able to feel the way the horse's hind legs are moving, which is the only way you can stay in harmony with him. The hind legs are where the horse begins his stride.

When you are seated properly in the saddle, you should not need your arms, legs, or knees to grab or control the horse. These parts of the body shouldn't to be used in an attempt to compensate for poor balance.

Your back should be straight but not stiff. Your arms should be kept your hands.

Your legs should be relaxed when you're seated properly on a horse. Your chin, hips, and heels should form a straight line, with your feet pointed forward. This is the classic three-point seat. When you are in this position, you will be in the horse's center of gravity and you should be able to easily adjust to the horse's actions.

The Improper Seat

A number of incorrect positions can be taken by a rider in the saddle, but there are three that are most common. All of them result in the rider becoming unbalanced and thus losing a great deal of control.

1. The chair seat: A position where the rider is sitting or leaning back too far. His knees become too elevated, pinching at the horse's sides rather than laying comfortably against them. The heels, instead of forming a straight line with the back, are too far forward, while the rider's back leans backward instead of remaining vertical.

2. Perching: The opposite of the chair seat, perching occurs when the rider has slid too far forward and his seat is up near the horse's neck. His back is no longer straight and his heels are elevated, with the toes pointing down instead of ahead.

Equine Tip

If you're out with your horse and encounter difficult weather such as rain, snow, or wind, be careful that you're not compensating for the conditions by altering your position in the saddle. This can cause you to lose your balance, upset the horse, and endanger both of you.

3. Slumping: This position occurs when the rider does not hold his head or neck straight but has let them hang forward, resulting in rounding his back and taking his seat bones out of the saddle. His arms are out in front instead of in their proper position near the rib cage.

Staying In Control

You have the proper seat, the horse is moving comfortably, and the two of you have started out on your journey. Now you need to maintain control of your horse. This requires utilizing all your equipment correctly. To do so, you need to use the aids, or cues, both natural and artificial, that are available to you. But don't forget that whether you're using your voice and body or your whip and spurs, you need to do so while maintaining the proper position.

Riding Vocab

The classic position for the rider is known as the three-point seat, which refers to the seat bones being in the saddle and two feet in the stirrups. When the rider is up out of the saddle as the horse picks up speed, the position is known as the two-point seat, meaning just the feet are still in the original position. This is also the position the rider will be in when the horse is going over jumps.

The forehand of the horse refers to the front legs, neck, shoulders, and withers.

Aids are the rider's resources while riding English-style. In western riding, aids are called cues. Natural aids or cues are a rider's voice, hands, and feet. Artificial aids are the equipment, including the reins, the bit, the saddle, the whip, and, the spurs.

Riding Vocab

Two terms used to describe the position of the reins while the horse is moving are long rein and loose rein. With a long rein, either the rider is pulling, trying to maintain control, or the horse is pulling forward, trying to run faster. The result is that the reins are stretched out further than normal.

With a loose rein, the rider has allowed the reins to slacken, letting the horse run at his own pace, sometimes known as on his own courage. The rider usually employs a loose rein when he is happy with the response he is getting from the horse and is satisfied with the speed at which they are going.

The Reins

The reins should be long enough to reach the rider comfortably, but not so long that they have to be gathered up and elevated. If the reins are too long and loose, they will lose connection with the horse's mouth and the rider will not be able to signal the horse through the bit. The reins should not be too tight around the horse's mouth or the horse will fight the rider and resist his directions.

There are several different ways to hold the reins. Your choice depends on the style of riding and type of bridle that you are using. Here are two ways to hold the reins:

1. The bridge grip: The rider grabs the reins either between the fourth and fifth fingers or outside of the fifth finger. The thumb holds the top of the reins.

2. The trainer's hold: A one-handed western grip that grabs the reins in the fist. The hand turns left or right depending on the steering direction being given. The reins are loose

enough that the rider can slide them up the horse's neck to signal a turn to the horse by touching either side.

The Bit

There are several ways the horse will respond to the pressures he feels in his mouth from the bit. If he's unhappy with the pressure, he'll usually respond by moving his head to try to stop it.

Above the bit is a term that describes an unhappy horse that is fighting the rider's commands by poking his nose out to try to resist the bit. This lifts the horse's head up and makes his back hollow. The best way to make the horse return to the correct position is by pulling back on the reins several times to slow and restrain him until he has returned his head to the proper position.

Behind the bit is another position of an unhappy horse. Instead of lifting his nose up, the horse moves it down toward his chest. The rider needs to press down on his seat while stiffening his back. This signals the horse to make the adjustment, but the rider must at the same time use his legs to keep the horse moving in stride.

If you have a happy horse that's responding to your commands and doesn't need more than light urging, he is described as being on the bit. This is the state you want to reach because it means the horse is pleased with the way you're riding him and wants to please you.

Riding Vocab

An expression used mostly in horse racing is spit the bit, which describes a horse that has stopped trying and no longer wants to compete.

English vs Western Riding Styles

The appearance of western riders and English riders couldn't be more different: the English rider, in his fancy, buttoned-down coat; the western rider, with a cowboy hat, jeans, and a rope in his hand. But there are many other differences between the two besides their appearance. They also train their horses differently. Certain signals from the rider mean one thing to an English-trained horse and another to a western-trained horse.

Steering

Western riders use their legs to steer their horses in any direction. Whereas English riders usually have to worry only about riding, western riders are frequently busy in the saddle performing other tasks. They can't always signal their horse with their hands. Western horses are trained to respond to body cues that English-trained horses wouldn't understand and would probably resent.

If you have a horse trained for English riding, wrapping with the arms or legs or kneeing the horse to get him moving in a certain direction won't work. Among the other problems these actions cause is that they make the horse feel that he's being restrained and his movements are being restricted. The horse's actions then become increasingly unsteady, which will make the rider feel even less balanced. In addition, whatever confidence the horse had in your control before the ride will go away quickly.

A horse trained for English riding will move in the direction that the reins are pulled. If the right rein is tugged, the horse turns to the right. This is known as moving toward the hand.

In western riding, when the rider touches the reins to the neck, the horse is trained to turn in the opposite direction. So if the horse feels a rein pressed on his right side, he turns left.

Holding the Reins

In English-style riding, the two reins are normally held one in each hand, though they are connected by a buckle. In western-style riding, the reins are held in just one hand, with the other hand free to hold a rope or some other object.

In English riding, the proper technique calls for the movements of the elbows to give the signals to the horse. As the elbows move, the reins move. Crooked wrists break the line between the elbows and the horse's mouth. When this happens, the signals that the rider is trying to give to the horse won't be communicated properly.

There are some western grips that require the rider to hold a lot more of the reins in his hands than is ever seen in English riding. One of these grips is known as the romel, which has the rider actually holding the reins straight up, with the excess parts of the reins allowed to drape over the side of the horse. This grip resembles the way you would hold an ice cream cone.

Making Good Decisions

You're out for a ride and you are in harmony with your horse. He's responding well to your commands and you've got all the equipment in the right place and functioning properly. Even so, it's still possible for you to mess up and turn what should be a fine experience into a bad one. This will happen if you suddenly make poor judgments that endanger you or your horse. In the process, you may well make the horse unhappy and turn what had been your cooperative partner into a defiant and unfriendly enemy.

Risky Paths

Even if you are an experienced rider, you must always be aware of the course that you're on. One example would be riding your horse on a path through trees. This type of route requires slower speeds to increase your margin of error. A horse can be spooked by a number of things in the woods, including hanging branches, falling leaves, and the sight or sounds of birds or animals.

Equine Tip

Do not smoke around your horse. Although tobacco companies used to have advertisements showing a cowboy riding with a cigarette in his mouth, it is not only dangerous to you, but your horse as well. You can get ashes in his eyes or nasal passages and you can burn him with a lit end. A horse will not trust you once you've hurt him with a cigar or cigarette.

Going too Fast

A typical ride requires many good judgments by the rider. One of these is the speed of the horse. It may be temporarily exhilarating, but the rider should never let his horse run at a speed faster than he is capable of controlling him. The horse is likely to feel a sense of freedom when he gets to go very fast, and the rider may find that when he tries to pull in the reins to slow him down, the horse won't respond to the bit. When this happens, the rider will frequently lose his seat and also have his feet come out of the stirrups, leaving him in a very precarious and dangerous position.

Uneven Ground

Another riding danger to be dealt with is steep terrain. Forcing a horse to go up a sharp hill is

Equine Tip

Wet, muddy, or snowy trails can be very slippery, which can cause the horse to fall and the rider to be thrown from the saddle. Puddles can also contain hidden dangers that aren't visible. The same is true of a road covered with snow.

A wet or slippery trail is best avoided or at least approached with much caution.

one of the most dangerous moves an inexperienced rider can make. The horse and rider can easily be thrown out of balance, creating danger for both of them.

Uncertain Ground

Occasionally, you may encounter a small bridge that may or may not be strong enough to hold you and your horse. Again, the best judgment is the cautious one. Either you need to find an alternate path or just turn around. There is no sense risking a whole lot of trouble that might come from a collapsed path or bridge.

Horse Sense

In addition to all of the immediate problems bad judgments can create, there are also the long-term effects on the relationship between you and your horse. If you've asked your horse to do something he didn't want to do, or if you led him into trouble, he is likely to lose trust in you. This is also true if you didn't sense that the horse was tired and you forced him to run on beyond his level of comfort. Once you've lost your horse's trust and confidence, it will be difficult to get it back.

Positive Results

If you avoid the wrong paths, maintain proper speed, and don't do anything that makes your horse mad or unfriendly, all your preparations and good judgment will pay off. Your rides will be experiences that are memorable not only for you, but for your horse, too. The next time you take him out, he'll recall the good time the two of you had before, and he'll be happy to head out with you again.

CHAPTER 13

 # The Horse in Motion

---

In This Chapter

➤ How a horse walks

➤ The faster gaits

➤ Fancy ambling

A horse moves with such grace and power that you may not notice that there is a certain rhythm to his strides. But in this chapter, you'll learn how each stride follows a pattern, almost like choreographed dance steps.

You'll learn about the five different types of strides from the slow walk to the fast gallop, and the many variations within each stride. You'll also learn about the many specialized steps of the amble, which certain breeds perform either in races or in competition.

You'll learn the proper ways to ride a horse depending on which stride he's employing. You'll also become familiar with the terms used to describe the horse's ways of moving and shifting his body.

The Walk

The walk is the slowest of the horse's strides, but it still has a rhythm and structure to it. Watch a horse walk and you'll notice a distinct four-beat stride—all four hooves land separately and in an orderly manner.

The walk is a lateral gait. The steps begin with a hind leg. If the left hind hits first, then the left front is next, followed by the right hind, and then the right front. If the right hind lands first, then the pattern is right-right, left-left.

Equine Tip

Whether you're utilizing an English or Western style, the basic techniques for riding all of the various strides of a horse are the same.

Riding the Walk

Once you're on your horse and you're ready to start walking, signal to him to start by squeezing with your feet. If that don't get him going, squeeze with your ankles. If he's still not moving, then use your voice to give him a verbal signal. Eventually, your horse should get the message.

Once you get your horse walking, use the first few minutes on his back to make sure that you're in a good position in the saddle. Make sure your seat bones are in the right spot. Try to keep your back straight and your elbows in the correct position.

When your horse is walking, you should be able to hear and feel his four steps. Make sure that they're in the correct order. If he's out of sequence, or if two feet land at the same time, it could cause him to lose his balance. If he has gotten out of step, squeeze with your legs to signal him to get into the correct rhythm and pattern.

The Trot

Unlike the walk, the trot is a diagonal stride and has a two-beat rhythm. The left front and the right hind step in unison, followed by the combination of the right front and left hind.

The most common way to make the transition from the walk to the trot is by picking up the horse's speed. As he starts walking faster, he should switch over to the trot.

A horse can go pretty fast in this stride. In fact, trotting races, contested at speeds of 30 miles an hour and more, have been quite popular around the world for centuries.

The Different Trots

There are four main variations of the trotting stride, and there is a natural progression to them:

1. Working trot: This is the most common trotting stride. Western riders utilize it when they are performing a variety of tasks, including herding. The horse's stride does not have great impulsion or collection during the working trot. The stride is steady, certainly faster than a walk, but not nearly as fast as a gallop.

2. Lengthening trot: This is a quicker trot that covers more ground at higher speeds. The rhythm of this variation is slower than the working trot because the strides are longer with more suspension. To get more length in the strides, the horse needs to generate more power, or impulsion, from his hindquarters.

Riding Vocab

Impulsion is the term used to describe the pushing power generated by a horse's hindquarters. The horse uses it to lengthen his strides and to increase his speed.

Collection is in many ways the opposite of impulsion. The weight is shifted to the hindquarters, while the power of the horse is shifted to its back and forehand, the part of the horse that is in front of the rider. Horses use collection to generate power before they elevate for a jump. The strides become shorter as the power is collected.

Suspension is the time in which the legs are in the air between each step. The more distance covered by a stride, the longer the suspension.

3. Medium trot: This is a more controlled stride than the lengthening trot, without as much reach and with greater collection. The horse bows his neck more noticeably during the medium trot, giving him a sublime appearance.

4. Extended trot: A horse in an extended trot reaches out further than he does in the other variations. It is similar to the lengthening trot but with even more impulsion. The horse also covers more ground, has a longer suspension, and reaches higher speeds than in any other type of trot.

Riding Vocab

Another variation of the trot is called the piaffe, which is seen in dressage competition. Basically, it is the trotting stride in place, with the horse moving forward very slightly. It requires great collection, with high elevation and suspension between the steps. The neck is heavily bowed.

The piaffe usually requires a good deal of training before a horse can master it, but when the piaffe is performed correctly, it's an impressive sight and is usually greatly appreciated by the audience.

Riding the Trot

Make sure that your back is straight when your horse is trotting. The lower part of the back is the only flexible part of the body that can absorb the horse's vibrations. If your back is arched and not straight, the lower back will get twisted too far when you get jolted and will knock you out of balance.

Leaning forward, or perching, makes it more difficult for the horse to generate power in his hindquarters, impeding his impulsion. Leaning back in the chair seat is uncomfortable for the horse, putting pressure on the wrong points as he's trying to move.

The Rising Trot

One of the ways to ride your horse when he is trotting is known as the rising trot, which is also referred to as posting.

There is a two-beat rhythm to the rising trot. You rise forward out of the saddle on the first beat, and then you settle back on the second beat.

You want to avoid coming down with your weight when the horse is lifting his inside leg. If he's turning to the left, have your weight come down when his right leg lands. Just reverse it when he's turning to the right.

If you get out of sequence during the rising trot, it's easy enough to change back. Just stay in the saddle for an extra beat, then lift up to be back in rhythm.

Equine Tip

When you're riding a trotting horse, it's a good idea to make frequent turns with him. This will get his attention and help keep him focused. Like young children, horses tend to get bored easily. If you ride them around the same circle several times, it will likely make them moody and uncooperative.

There are more good reasons for making turns when you're riding the sitting trot. When you stay in place on a horse's back for a while, his muscles will tighten up a bit. The shifting of the turns will make him feel like he's loosened up and can extend his stride.

The Sitting Trot

A sitting trot is when you don't bounce in the saddle while the horse is trotting. Your legs should be straight, so before you start moving, make sure that you've adjusted the stirrups to the right length.

The Canter

The canter has elements of both the controlled stride of the trot and the mostly unrestrained gallop. While the walk is four beats and the trot is two, the canter is three beats.

You need to be seated and not bouncing on your horse when you make the transition from the trot to the canter. Normally, the horse makes the transition if you increase his speed.

The canter starts with a back foot. If the horse is on his right lead, the stride begins when he pushes off with the back left foot, then the left front and back right land in unison. Finally, the right front lands and pulls, or leads, the horse forward.

The decision as to which lead to be on depends on the direction you and your horse are going (this is true whether your horse is in a gallop or on the canter). If you're turning left, you'll want the left lead. If you're in a closed circle, you'll want to be on the lead that brings you and your horse toward the center.

Different Variations of the Canter

Much like the trot, there are several versions of the canter. The progression is also pretty similar to the trotting variations. The canter begins with the standard working canter, followed by the medium canter, which gives the horse more impulsion and longer strides. The collected canter gives the horse less impulsion, shorter strides, and, naturally, more collection. The next progression is the extended canter, which, like the extended trot, gives the horse longer strides and more suspension.

The fastest stride of the canter is called the hand gallop. Though the horse is going faster, he doesn't go fast enough to break into a full gallop, maintaining his three-beat stride.

The lope is a variation of the canter used primarily in western riding. It gives a horse more collection and is slower than the regular canter.

Riding the Canter

To ride the canter, you should be upright and leaning back slightly with your back relaxed. If you lean forward while your horse is cantering, it will cause him to go faster than you want.

You should be upright with your back relaxed and leaning back slightly during this stride. Don't speed up your rhythm, either, since that will also make the horse go faster than you want.

Move your hips in rhythm with the horse. You want to keep your seat bones in the saddle. If you want your horse to go faster, you can signal this to him by moving your hips forward. To stop the horse, just stop moving your hips while you pull back lightly on the reins.

The Gallop

A galloping horse is usually reaching out for maximum speed. When walking, the horse is going about 4 miles an hour. When he is in a full gallop, he could reach speeds over 40 miles an hour.

Like the walk, the gallop is a four-beat stride, but with a different sequence. If the horse is on a left lead, the right hind foot lands first followed by the left hind foot, then the right front, and finally the left front.

When some champion race horses are in a full gallop, they have tremendous suspension. Their strides can reach out to 30 feet, more than three times their own length. These horses have tremendous impulsion from their hindquarters, which sends them flying forward.

Riding the Gallop

Because of the high speeds, there is too much danger for inexperienced riders to let their horse gallop. Do not try it until you have mastered the canter.

You should never ask your horse to gallop in an enclosed area. The horse not only needs a lot of room to run, but also to slow down. Horses that are galloping at high speeds usually need at least a ¼ mile before they come to a full stop.

When you make the transition from the canter to the gallop, you need to lean forward and lift up out of the saddle into the two-point position and shorten your reins, which will give you more control at the higher speed. You should also pick up the pace of your riding by moving your hands more rapidly and forcefully. This will signal to the horse that you want him to move faster.

If you need to slow the horse down or make an unplanned stop, just lean back with your weight while pulling back the reins.

Galloping puts a lot of strain on a horse's body, so even if you've become experienced and skillful enough to ride it, don't do it too often.

You want to use the gallop only during the outward part of your trip. Riding home at a gallop is likely to make the horse much harder to control because he'll want to rush back to his stall and his food.

The Amble

The amble is usually a faster version of the walk, often with fancy trained steps. The progression of steps of the amble can be either lateral (left-left, right-right) or diagonal (left-right, left-right).

The Lateral Gaits

Though the amble is usually not as fast as the trot or canter, there are some exceptions. Certain breeds that employ the lateral-gaited amble can move very fast. When a Paso Fino, a popular breed in Latin America and South America, is ambling, he can reach speeds close to 30 miles an hours. His legs move rapidly, and you can hear his hooves rattling like castanets.

The Running Walk

There are some strides that are variations to the basic walk, most notably, the running walk. Like the standard walk, the running walk is a lateral gait, but as you might guess from the name, it's a quicker version.

When horses are walking, there is a natural over-stride, which means that their hind legs land beyond the hoof prints left by the front legs. In the running walk, the over-stride is even more pronounced, up to two feet ahead of the front steps. This lets the horse cover more ground and move faster even though his stride is not any quicker.

The most famous demonstration of the running walk is performed by the Tennessee walking horse. Its front steps are very high, with the legs curled up in the air. A lot of training and practice is required for the members of this breed to perform these steps properly. This entertaining use of the running walk has made the Tennessee walking horse quite popular for both riding and exhibitions.

The Spanish Walk

This gait is distinctive and easy to notice. The horse lifts his front legs very high and forward with each step. The front leg almost reaches the height of the horse's chin. The gait is similar to the running walk employed by the Tennessee walking horse, but it is usually not as fast and the leg does not curl.

Several Spanish breeds are taught to perform this stride, including the Andalusian, which is often seen in horse shows or even in circuses and carnivals. Wherever it is performed, the Spanish walk is a real crowd pleaser.

The Pace

The pace is the fastest of the lateral-gaited ambles. Race horses can travel up to 35 miles an hour while pacing. It is a two-beat stride, with both left-side legs landing at the same time followed by the right legs.

Pacers are sometimes called side-wheelers because their two-beat action seems to bounce them back and forth rapidly from left to right.

The Rack

The rack is another of the specialized lateral strides. It is similar to the pace, except that there are four beats. Horses utilizing the rack can reach speeds close to those obtained by pacers. The rack requires the horse to have both high and rapid leg action.

There is a specific breed that specializes in the rack, known, fittingly, as the racking horse. But the American saddlebred is the most famous and certainly the most popular breed that specializes in the rack.

The Slow Gaits

In addition to the walk, trot, canter, and rack, the versatile American saddlebred, a rare five-gaited horse, can perform versions of the slow gaits. These are lateral gaits particularly noted for their smoothness.

One of these strides is called the single-foot, which is a four-beat gait. Another is the stepping pace, which has also four beats, but, unlike the single-foot, the beats are not evenly paced. There is an extra pause between the second and third steps.

The Tolt

This is a specialized gait of horses from Scandinavia and Iceland. It is a lateral gait reminiscent of the rack, but the steps are less restricted and the strides are longer. The tölt also features high lift in the forelegs.

Icelandic horses that employ the tölt can reach high speeds while still maintaining a very smooth ride.

The Paso Fino

Paso Fino translates from the Spanish to mean "fine steps." It is a breed from Puerto Rico and Colombia that employs several versions of the lateral-gaited amble. The fanciest version is actually named the Paso Fino, and it is made up of rapid, short steps and is seen primarily in show competitions.

The Paso Fino utilizes other versions of the amble as well. They are the passo corto, used primarily for pleasure riding, and the passo largo, in which the horse's steps are much longer and faster than in the passo corto.

The Diagonal Gaits

There are not as many breeds that employ the diagonal gait of the amble compared to the lateral gaits. The lateral gaits are considered to be easier on the horse since both sides of the body absorb the weight of each stride.

The Fox Trot

The Missouri fox trotter is perhaps the most famous horse, at least in North America, to utilize a diagonal-gaited amble. It is bred and trained for a specific gait, known as the fox trot.

Unlike a regular trot, there is a four-beat rhythm to the fox trot. It is an uneven rhythm as well. After the first two steps, there is a slight pause before the third and fourth steps. This eliminates much of the bounce for the rider, giving him a smoother trip. The horse's head is also very active during the fox trot, bobbing up and down, with the neck also moving quite a bit.

Horse Sense

It's no surprise that most of the horses that employ a fancy amble require firm, hard surfaces. In particular, the horses of Latin America and South America, the Paso Fino and the Mangalarga Marchador, are raised in areas with firmer conditions.

The fast steps of the Paso Fino, for instance, work best on hard pavement or firm roads, where the horse can move his feet rapidly. These strides would not work well on softer grounds and certainly not in wintry conditions.

The Tennessee walking horse also needs firm ground to perform the steps of its fancy running walk. Even the horses from northern climates that perform the steps of the tölt require firm, clear roads that have had all ice and snow removed.

The Trocha and Marcha Batida

There are some breeds from South America that use strides similar to the fox trot. Many of the Paso Fino raised in Colombia have been trained to develop a lateral gait called the trocha. It is similar to the fox trot and another fancy ambling stride, the marcha batida.

The marcha batida is the lateral gait of the Mangalarga Marchador, a popular horse in South America, specifically in Brazil, where they number in the hundreds of thousands.

PART FOUR

Equine Activities

CHAPTER 14

Western Sports

In This Chapter

➤ Barrel races

➤ Reining competitions

➤ Western pleasure events

➤ Equitation

In this chapter, you'll learn about several sports that utilize the traditions of western riding. You'll learn about the fast competitions of barrel racing and the fancy moves of reining. You'll learn about the specialized presentations of western pleasure and how riders compete in western equitation.

Barrel Racing

Barrel racing is considered one of the activities in western riding that is the most fun, and many riding academies offer training in the sport for their new riders. The rules are not particularly complicated. Barrels are set up around a course and the horse that makes its way around the course the fastest wins. The course is set up small enough so that events can take place at indoor arenas.

History of the Sport

Barrel racing was originally introduced into western competitions in Texas during the 1930s as an event for women. While men were doing more power-based activities like roping and steer riding, the women at rodeos were there primarily for show. There had been women at Wild West exhibitions for more than fifty years, doing trick riding and target shooting. Annie Oakley was the most famous of the women at these shows but not the only one.

At most rodeos, women were given prizes based on the appearance of their horses and the attractiveness of their own costumes. The prizes usually weren't paid out in cash, but in gifts considered appropriate for women such as hair and makeup items.

Barrel racing was devised as a way for women to show off their own qualities of horsemanship in events that didn't require great strength. Eventually, women formed their own rodeo associations independent of the men, and some of the events that were thought inappropriate for women were gradually added. But barrel racing remains the most popular event.

Winning a Race

Originally, barrel races were decided not just by the fastest time, but by the look of the horse and the style of the rider. That's all changed. Barrel racing is now strictly a race against the clock.

The one exception to this are match races. There is an entire circuit of events dedicated to this form of barrel racing. Two identical courses are set up for the two competitors, and the first one past the finish line wins. There is no timing required.

Match races are held like tournaments are held in most any other sport, with quarterfinals and semifinals leading to a championship match. In some competitions, the match races are held outdoors on courses much larger than the standard setup found in arenas.

The Course

Barrel racing does not take very long. The course is short enough that most races take less than fifteen seconds, with the world record time for negotiating a course just over thirteen seconds. There are some special events where the course is larger and horse and rider need about twice as long to negotiate it. There are other special events where some of the barrels are either removed or arranged differently.

In a standard race, the barrels themselves must be at least 55 gallons and closed. Each barrel has to be at least two colors. This is in deference to the horse having problems with depth perception.

Usually, barrel races take place on a sand or dirt course, though occasional outdoor events are set up on grass. This is considered to be less favorable for the horse, since grass can be slipperier than dirt. But there are some annual rodeos that have been in business for a long time and they can't or won't change their grass course. Most professional riders avoid these grass courses because of the potential danger.

There is no official course for barrel racing, but there is a conventional course setup. The original course was set up in a figure-eight pattern. Later, that was thought to be too easy, so a cloverleaf pattern was established, which then became the standard.

The barrels are set up in a triangle pattern, with the rider beginning from the start-finish line 45 feet in front of the first two barrels. Horse and rider enter the arena at high speed and cross the start line to begin the timing of their race. In the past, a man with a flag gave the signal to start the time as the horse crossed the line, but now the timing is all done with electronic eyes.

Horse and rider then head for the first barrel, which is on the lower right side of the triangle. The rider then circles the barrel from the left side, making his circle around the obstacle in a clockwise manner. Horse and rider then head to the second barrel, which is 90 feet away.

The second barrel is circled counterclockwise from the right side. After finishing the loop, horse and rider head up to the third barrel, which is 105 feet away at the top of the triangle. This barrel is also circled counterclockwise.

Once they are around the third barrel, they head back to the finish line, staying between the first two barrels, to register their final time.

If a horse fails to execute a turn correctly, he is disqualified; if he bumps into one of the barrels, there is a five-second penalty.

For the safety of horse and rider, there has to be at least 60 feet behind the finish line before the space in the arena runs out. There also must be at least 15 feet from the side of the arena to each of the first two barrels. At least 30 feet from the third barrel to the back of the arena is also required.

Equine Tip

The saddle used in barrel racing has a square seat specifically designed for the sport. It also has a deep skirt. It is a lighter saddle, which allows the horse to reach high speeds while turning. If you're barrel racing, be sure to adjust the stirrups so they are very high, which will allow the horse to ride at faster speeds.

Riding in Races

The key to barrel racing is not just speed, but also the ability to make turns quickly. Barrel racing is as much a technical event as it is a speed event. Usually, the horse that makes its circles as close to the barrels as possible has the fastest time and wins the race.

It's important during a race that the rider doesn't start turning his horse too early or too late. If he does, he won't be in the right position at the turn and there's a very good chance the horse will hit the barrel.

Another important tip is for the rider to keep a straight line when going from one barrel to the next. He'll give himself all sorts of problems if he starts veering off the best path. Not only will he add distance to his journey, but he'll have to lose speed in order to correct his line going into a turn.

The more time you spend riding in barrel races, the better you will get. It's okay for someone to tell you how to do it, but in reality, you need experience to know how much pressure to apply with the legs or how much to turn the reins.

Competing in Barrel Racing

There is a lot of money in barrel racing for the fastest horses. The Barrel Racing Association offers millions of dollars of purses for the best racers. As a result, the best barrel racing horses sell for large sums of money.

However, the sport is not just for the fastest and the most expensive. Virtually any horse you have, from a pony to a large cold-blooded horse, can be trained to participate in the fun of the sport.

A big horse such as a Clydesdale can't get around the turns as fast as smaller breeds, but if that's the type of horse you have, you can still have fun training your horse for barrel racing and riding him around a course, even if it takes him a long time to finish.

Reining

The sport of reining is similar to other western sports since it is derived from the skills and maneuvers used by riders in the old days of the West. Unlike many other western sports, there are no cattle involved in reining, though many of the movements used were ones that were needed to handle cattle.

Both the rider and the horse are judged and rated in the sport of reining. There are a designated series of moves that must be performed. Depending on the competition, the number of required moves is between eight and twelve. All moves are performed either at a gallop or a lope, the slow western version of the canter. The scoring is open-ended, though the average score, as in most horse competitions, is 70.

In most reining events, the horse uses a curb bit. In some events, especially those for younger horses, a hackamore, the bridle with no bit, is permitted.

The Moves

Horses are required to run in perfect circles. The horse must make a large circle while in a full gallop, and a smaller circle while on a lope. Part of the scoring of reining is the transition the horse makes from the gallop to the lope.

Lead Changes

The horse needs to make smooth changes from one lead foot to the other when he changes directions. The maneuver should be done quickly and with all four legs in unison.

Rundown, Sliding Stop, and Rollback

A horse enters the arena by making a rundown, which is a run or gallop just off the arena fenceat high speed. After coming to a stop, he then performs the slow canter, or lope, before he then he goes into the sliding stop in which his hind feet are planted and skidding (not stepping) forward. The front legs continue to walk forward until the full stop is executed, usually in a cloud of dust.

After the horse has completed his sliding stop, he turns around immediately and starts loping in the opposite direction. This is known as the rollback.

Backups, Spins, and Pauses

The reining horse is required to walk backward for at least 10 feet at a fairly quick pace while keeping his body perfectly straight.

Another maneuver required in reining calls for the horse to spin around in place. As many as four full revolutions are executed in spins. During his presentation, each horse must spin in both directions. If the horse has not made enough spins or has made too many, points will be deducted from his score.

A horse is expected to pause after certain movements, including the execution of spins. There is no scoring of the pauses unless the horse is marked down for being ill-behaved during the segment.

Scoring

The judges can mark deductions of ½ point up to 5 points. An egregious fault, such as the horse leaving the course or going off pattern, means performing the movements out of sequence, and the horse and rider can be disqualified.

Extra points are awarded if the horse executes an excellent maneuver. The judge's cards are collected after each horse and, naturally, the highest score wins.

Reining Equipment

The reining saddle allows the rider to sit deeply in the seat. It has longer fenders, which enable the rider to swing his legs more freely so he can give the horse added directions during competition.

Horses wear special shoes called slide plates for reining competition. Slide plates make it easier for the horse to perform a sliding stop.

Reining Quarter Horses

Like most western sports, the American quarter horse, with its strong legs that give it speed and maneuverability, has developed to be the ideal breed for reining competition. The sanctioning group for the breed, the American Quarter Horse Association (AQHA), was the first to recognize reining as a sport in 1949. Since then, the sport has spread to many breeds and many countries, not to mention many equine organizations, both national and international. In 2012, reining became a part of the World Equestrian Games.

The breeding of reining horses can be a lucrative business, with hundreds of stallions standing around the country at stud. Breeding rights to a reining stallion are usually priced between $500 and $1,000, with the top stallions standing for a little more.

Freestyle Reining

A recent development is the creation of freestyle reining events, which are done to music.

In many ways, freestyle reining resembles the old Wild West shows of the past (and occasionally the present). There are some requirements as far as the number of spins and stops, but otherwise, there is a lot of artistic freedom. Competitors are allowed to set up props in the arena. They can also use special lighting and wear fancy costumes.

The judging of freestyle reining is done on artistic and technical merit, as well as on entertainment. Sometimes the audience also gets to vote through an applause meter.

Western Pleasure

While the action in most western sports goes off at a rapid pace, western pleasure is designed to be a much more leisurely competition. The horse is judged by his calmness and the ease of his movements.

The official rules for western pleasure, as listed by the AQHA, explains the correct manners of a horse in competition: "A good pleasure horse has a free-flowing stride of reasonable length … while exhibiting correct gaits that are of the proper cadence … . He should carry his head and neck in a relaxed, natural position."

Horses are judged on three different gaits: the walk, the jog, which is a very slow version of the trot, and the lope. The rider should not be tugging hard on the reins while the horse is moving about during his presentation. The horse should appear collected and move smoothly. At the signal from the judge, the horse should move from one end of the arena to the other. There are designated pauses as well as moments when the horse is asked to move backward.

The Show

During an event, all the horses in the competition parade in the arena ring at the same time and periodically go through their paces together. At other points, individual horses move by themselves.

Like most western sports, the average score in the event is 70. There are a number of faults that can be marked against a horse. Too much speed is one mark down, as is not performing a stride properly.

Most important in the judging is the position of the horse's head. Though the head should be low, it shouldn't be so far down that the ears are below the withers.

Breeds in Competition

At the highest competitive level of the sport, each breed has its own competition and champion. But most western pleasure events are mixed-breed events. As always seems to be the case with western competitions, the quarter horse is the most successful breed, but the Appaloosa, the paint, and the Morgan have also had success.

Horse Sense

Many other breeds not usually associated with western sports have also been a part of western pleasure events. Even the breeds with the fanciest strides, including the Tennessee walking horse and the Missouri fox trotter, have been involved in the sport.

Western Equitation

Western equitation is quite similar to western pleasure, though the horse is not necessarily going about in a leisurely manner, as in the other discipline. Equitation is also more about the rider than the horse. It is the rider's position in the saddle and the positions that he guides the horse into that are being judged.

The three strides used are the same as in western pleasure, the walk, the jog, and the lope. Similar to dressage in English riding, there is a whole series of moves the rider must make, and he is given a score for each one.

There are patterns that the horse must execute, such as a circle and a figure eight. There are also transitions between strides that require lead changes. Some of the moves used in reining are also utilized in equitation events, such as full spins and the rollback.

Equitation Saddle

The saddle used in western equitation competitions is built with a very deep seat to hold the rider in place. There are also heavy fenders, which prevent the legs from moving excessively. Another difference in an equitation saddle is that the horn is not as high as it is on most western saddles.

Scoring

The judges look closely at the rider. They will judge him on his posture in the saddle, which should be upright. The judges will also look at the position of the hand that is holding the reins. The hand should be close to the rider's body and centered over the horse's body.

Another consideration is the position of the rider's legs. If they are angled forward or backward, the judges will assume that the rider does not have adequate control of his horse.

CHAPTER 15

Horse and Cattle Sports

In This Chapter

➤ Separating cattle

➤ Roping steers

➤ Roping cattle

In this chapter, you'll learn about the western sports involving horses and cattle. These are all closely associated with the popular rodeos that tour the United States and Canada. You'll learn about penning and cutting, two sports that involve separating cattle from the herd. You'll learn about the teamwork required to succeed in both sports. You'll also learn about calf roping and steer roping, two popular and lucrative western sports.

Cutting

Cutting's roots go back to the cowboys of the West. As with most western sports, cutting is simple. The horse and rider are required to separate a member of cattle from a herd and keep them separated for a while.

Cutting is one of the western events that has evolved into a lucrative sport. The richest events in the sport are worth many millions of dollars, and there is more than $30 million in annual prize money for events sponsored by the National Cutting Horse Association (NCHA).

Cutting History

Cutting was an activity of cowboys in the West long before it became a sport. In the nineteenth century, cattle needed to be separated from the herd for various reasons, and cutting horses were used to do the separating. There soon developed arguments over what horse and what rider were the best at cutting. Ranchers would seek out the best cutters and reward them for their work.

In 1898, in Texas, the first organized cutting competitions were developed. The sport continued to grow through the West until the NCHA was formed after World War II. The sport has continued to grow in the subsequent decades until it has reached the large and lucrative level that it now enjoys.

Cutting Saddle

The saddle used for this competition is constructed with a deep seat. This allows the rider to adjust quickly while directing the horse through the sharp turns that need to be negotiated in this type of western activity. There is also a high horn that can be used to give the horse added direction.

Cutting Competition

In a competition, the rider has 2½ minutes to show the horse. Ideally, the horse herds with little help from the rider. This is demonstrated by the rider having a loose rein, which means he is not offering much direction to his horse.

The well-trained cutting horse learns to anticipate the moves of the cattle, whose instinct is to get back with its herd. The horse keeps moving back and forth, preventing the bovine from returning to the group until it turns away. At that point, the horse and rider choose another animal to separate from the herd and repeat the process.

Usually, three cows are worked in the 2½ minutes, though sometimes only two are used. The rider must get at least one cow from the back of the herd.

Other riders, called herd holders, keep the rest of the herd grouped, which makes it easier for the cutting horse to perform his task.

The horse and rider are given a score based on their success. The range of scoring is from 60 to 80 points for each judge. Much of the scoring is subjective, based on the judge's view of the horse's performance. The degree of difficulty of the cow is one factor in the judging, as is the way the horse controlled the cow.

Equine Tip

Part of the scoring of the judges in cutting is based on the courage shown by the horse and the degree to which the horse acted on his own without much direction from the rider. That's why participants in the sport of cutting want to get horses that show a particular interest in working with cattle, which is not a common trait.

There are some parts of scoring that are not subjective. If the cow gets too close to the back fence, the horse is penalized 3 points. There is also a deduction if the rider fails to make the more difficult deep cut from the back of the herd. Other deductions or even disqualifications come for leaving the area early, dismounting the horse, or being forced from the seat. Cruel treatment of the horse also results in disqualification.

The Events

The sport, like most western events, is also popular in western Canada, which has its own organized group, the Canadian Cutting Horse Association (CCHA). The CCHA was formed in Calgary, Alberta, just three years after the NCHA was formed in Texas. The Canadian season stretches from the spring into the fall, with events throughout the provinces of Alberta, Manitoba, and British Columbia.

Though there are many areas and regions of the country that have cutting events, most of the sanctioned events in the sport take place in the original home state of cutting, Texas. This includes the biggest event in the sport, the Futurity, which is held annually in the autumn in Fort Worth.

Horse Sense

Cutting is clearly a sport of the American West. Though there are events in Georgia and Florida as well as the northern plains, most of the NCHA competitions take place in Texas and other southwestern and western states.

Cutting horse competitions are broken down into several categories:

> ➤ Professional: For anyone who has received payment for working in any equine activity

> ➤ Nonprofessional: For those who have never received payment for working in any equine activity

> ➤ Amateur: For all riders who have earned $100,000 or less in open cutting competitions. The total is $50,000 in earnings from the less lucrative Weekend and Limited Age events.

Young People

In addition to the events for adults, there is also a National Youth Cutting Horse Association, which sanctions events that are open to all under age eighteen.

Cutting is considered a good activity for youth because it requires teamwork, patience, and focus, as well as time management.

Cutting Horses

All breeds are welcome to compete in cutting competitions, according to the rules of the NCHA. "In any NCHA class," says the rulebook, "competition must be open to any horse, regardless of breed, age, sex, color, conformation, appearance or previous performance." This line is then added to the rule: "Horses are judged on performance only." In other words, a judge shouldn't discriminate based on his preference of breed.

Even so, most of the best cutting horses are American quarter horses. The best quarter horse cutting horses are sold for big money for their breeding rights.

The Cattle

All of the cattle used in cutting competitions have never been involved in any event before. Young cattle are generally preferred, one- or two-year-olds. All the cattle used must weigh at least 500 pounds.

Before the Event

The organization putting on a cutting event is required to have an area where the horse can be worked out or loped before the show. It is also required to have good ground in both the loping pen and in the competition area. This means ground that is not too hard or slick. The course is made up of sand and should be free of rocks and other hard pieces such as gravel.

A tractor is used to drag the ground to keep it firm and even. This is true both in the loping pen and in the main area.

Penning

Like cutting, penning has its roots in ranch work and was later turned into a sport. Also like cutting, penning involves separating cattle from the herd. In this case, it is three designated head of cattle, and they are directed by a team of three riders, each with equal work.

Penning was created as a sport in 1942. The first organized events took place in California in 1949. The sanctioning body of the sport is the United States Team Penning Association (USTPA). In addition, there are many local team penning groups that hold weekly or monthly events for local riders.

The tradition of the sport, wherever and whenever a competition is held, is that the winners of events are presented with valuable buckles, the value depending on the importance of the event.

Rules of Team Penning

A herd of thirty young cattle is used. Ten of them are each wearing a number from zero to nine on its back. A random draw determines which of the numbered cattle each competing team will need to separate. When the first rider of a team crosses the starting line, the numbers of the three cattle are announced, both to the crowd and to the riders.

The three numbered cattle must be separated from the herd. Then they are brought down to the opposite end of the arena, where they must be put through a 10-foot opening of a pen that is 16 by 24 feet.

Race Against the Clock

The three riders of each team must work together. Once they have separated the three cattle from the herd, the rider furthest from the pen is called the "sweep," since he is most responsible for moving the cattle forward, or sweeping them ahead and out of the herd. The middle rider is known as the "wing," since he is most responsible for moving the cattle down to the pen. The rider nearest the pen is called the "hole," which is the common term for the opening into the pen. While the three cattle are driven forward, the remaining cattle, referred to as trash cattle, must be kept back.

After the three cattle are in the pen, the first rider across the line into the pen lifts his hat to signal for the time to stop. The time limit is from sixty to ninety seconds, depending on the level of the competition. The very best teams often get all the work done in less than thirty seconds, sometimes less than twenty seconds.

There are other rules to team penning. There is a foul line ¾ of the way toward the pen, and only one wrong-numbered cattle may go past that line. If there is more than one wrong-numbered cattle past the foul line, the team is disqualified. The team is also disqualified if a wrong-numbered animal enters the pen.

Roping

Like the other western sports, the various events involving roping are based on the activities of the cowboys of the West. Not only was it necessary to separate cattle from the herd, as in cutting and penning, but it was also necessary to capture them after they got loose. The sports involving roping are all variations of capturing cattle.

There are two main forms of roping, one involving two riders, the other just one. In most cases, they are racing against the clock.

A good deal of prize money can be won in roping. There are lucrative events held throughout the year. The best riders in any of these sports can earn hundreds of thousands of dollars in a year.

Breeding Roping Horses

There is big money to be had in breeding roping horses. The top sires in these sports can command stud fees in the thousands. Championship horses and sires can sell for several hundred thousand dollars, even millions.

Riding Vocab

Standing is the term used for a stallion at stud. The stud fee of a horse is just a small part of his value. Since a stud can produce a hundred or more offspring a year, the value of the horse is around one hundred times his stud fee. So if a horse is standing for $1,000, his actual value is probably about $100,000. The value can change depending on the age of the stallion and the breed.

The primary breeding state for roping stallions is Texas, but there are also many breeding farms located in California, Nebraska, Wisconsin, Oklahoma, and Montana.

The popularity of the quarter horse in roping sports is evident by their numbers at breeding farms. The number of roping stallions that are quarter horses is more than ten times higher than that of the next most popular breed.

Roping Saddle

The specific saddle used by riders in roping sports is unusually heavy, made sturdy to accommodate the rider's actions. It also includes a thicker horn, designed to wrap a large rope around it. The horn is big enough that a large steer can be tied to it securely.

The roping saddle comes with a fork swell for quicker dismounting so the rider can get to the cattle he's roped.

Team Roping

In team roping, a large steer is released from a chute into the arena ring, and are followed by two riders with ropes. They are known as the header and the heeler. As the steer enters, the header and the heeler move toward it from opposite directions. The header tries to lasso the steer around the horns, around the neck, or around both the horns and neck. Once he has executed the maneuver, the heeler tries to loop the hind legs of the steer. When he does this successfully and the animal is stretched out unable to move, the clock is stopped. The steer is then untied and released.

The fastest time usually wins, though there are other competitions with multiple rounds that don't time the runs, but just count the successful throws.

During most team roping events where time is the deciding factor, extra seconds are added for each mistake. If only one hind leg was roped by the heeler, there is a five-second penalty. In some competitions, if the first throw misses, the rider tries again to rope the steer. At the highest levels of competition, there is only one throw allowed.

The best team ropers can complete their efforts in just a few seconds. The world record is less than three seconds.

Steer Roping

Steer roping is similar to team roping but involves only one rider. The steer is released into the arena wearing a light rope, which then breaks when it gets to the end. This releases the gate and allows the horse and rider to enter the ring. If the rider enters early, there is a ten-second penalty.

The rider throws the rope around the steer's neck to pull him to the ground. The rider then dismounts and goes to the steer as his horse continues to move forward.

The rider ties three of the steer's legs together, and then returns to his horse and releases the rope. If the steer stays tied for six seconds, then the judge calls time and the roping is considered successful. The fastest time wins.

Calf Roping

Calf roping is pretty much the same as steer roping other than it involves a young animal rather than a full-sized bovine. There are other slight variations as well. The rider throws a rope around the neck of the calf, and then dismounts from the horse. Unlike steer roping, the horse is brought to a stop before the rider gets off and the calf has to be upright before the rider can tie its legs. If the calf has been knocked over, then the rider has to pick it up before it knocks it down again. A variation of the sport is breakaway roping, where the calf stays on its feet.

The fastest time wins and in major competitions, the fastest time is usually about seven seconds.

Big Money

The top earners in all the roping sports can earn a lot of money year after year. The top competitors in each discipline have career earnings well into the millions. There are many major roping events throughout the year, usually in conjunction with organized rodeos.

CHAPTER 16

English Riding Sports

> ## In This Chapter
>
> ➤ Dressage competitions
> ➤ Jumping fundamentals
> ➤ Cross-country racing
> ➤ Hunt seat shows

In this chapter, you'll learn about the many English equestrian sports that involve show rings and jumping. You'll learn about the elegant sport of dressage. You'll learn about the many jumping sports and the proper form needed to clear hurdles. And you'll also learn about hunters and jumpers, the horses that compete in hunt seat competitions.

Dressage

Dressage is a fancy term for, well, making you and your horse look pretty fancy. This is why dressage has a reputation as being the way the wealthy and the powerful ride to fill their leisure time. That may well be true, but it doesn't diminish the value or the pleasure of taking part in the activity of dressage.

The term itself is a French word that translates simply to mean a form of training. The basics of dressage can be utilized in any other kind of riding.

Though control of the horse is still important, there is more of an emphasis on appearance in dressage that most other forms of riding do not have. Form and style matter, and in competition, horses are required to stride exactly the right way to get the perfect score.

There is a great deal of elegance to the sport of dressage. The appearance is of a pristine horse and rider. The horse is—or should be—perfectly groomed and is often dappled up from mane to tail. The rider also looks very smart in a long black coat with white britches. But despite the appearance in the ring, there is a lot of sweat and toil required before the dressage rider and horse can succeed.

Equine Tip

Training for dressage is time-consuming and requires a certain type of horse that is both cooperative and athletic. The rider also must develop a great deal of patience to train his horse for the many moves and stops required in a presentation. Horse and rider need time together to be in sync, since much of the scoring in the event is based on the rider having the trust of his horse.

The Dressage Equipment

A dressage saddle has wide flaps designed for the purpose of keeping the rider balanced. This is done not only for safety, but to help the rider maintain proper form, which is so important in competition.

Dressage does not include jumping, so the saddle is constructed for the legs to reach further down. This also makes it easier for the rider to signal to the horse with his legs.

The dressage saddle is not designed for speed. The seat is also deeper than that of most English saddles.

The other equipment used includes a snaffle bridle and bit. A pelham bit, which includes both snaffle and curb bits, is also used.

The Competition

Dressage competitions are broken down according to the level or age of both the horses and the riders. There are also events for specific breeds of horses as well as for ponies.

In the Show Ring

Dressage horses and riders compete in tests, a scheduled series of moves that are written on a card and given to the rider before the event. The rider does not know what the exact requirements of his test will be until the day of the event, so he has to be prepared for any demand. The tests require the horse to move in designated strides, making transitions between the strides, and to perform other movements, such as circles and lateral movements.

Halts and half-halts are important in dressage, as is the proper form of the horse's body. Depending on the stride, the horse is expected to show excellent technical form, be it impulsion or collection. The rider is also graded on the way that the horse responds to his commands. If a rider needs great urging to get his mount to execute a maneuver, that is given a mark down.

Riding Vocab

A half-halt is not a full halt, or stop, but a change of tempo as a horse changes strides. In dressage, the half-halt should be evident in the stride transition.

As the horse performs his routine, the judges rate each move according to a prescribed standard. The scoring goes from 0 for a move not executed to 10 for perfect execution. There are plenty more 0s given out than 10s. A very good score is about 70 points for ten movements.

Judges write their scores down on a card as the competitor goes through his test. This is known as scribing. The judges also write comments about each move that explain their scoring and can be used as an aid by the rider after his test is over.

At the lowest level among beginning riders and horses, the moves are usually quite limited and simple. As the level of competition increases, the movements become increasingly difficult.

Jumping

Other than dressage, almost all other types of English equestrian show events involve jumping. There are more than twenty variations to the obstacles that are set up on courses in arenas and cross-country competitions. They vary in height, length, width, and thickness. The jumps are designed to be taken at different speeds and require the jumping horse to display a variety of skills.

Sometimes, the horse jumps the whole obstacle at once. Other times, he may be required to leap more than once over an obstacle. This could involve taking steps between the hurdles or, as in a coffin jump, leaping over one fence and then going over the other without taking a step.

A drop fence jump sees the horse landing at a spot much lower than the level where the jump began. A sunken road jump is set in an opposite way, with the horse clearing a jump to land at a higher elevation.

The jumps are made of many materials, including wood and stone. If a jump is made of very solid material and cannot be knocked over, usually a horse is not given faults for touching it. Depending on the competition, the less sturdy jumps usually must be cleared without any contact.

Many jumps are made of brush, which are often set higher than rails. The brush is set on top of a solid base. Usually, as with a bullfinch jump, the horse is supposed to go through the brush, rather than leap over it.

There are other jumps, such as a drop fence, in which the horse lands at a different height from the ground on the other side of the jump. This requires good balance from the horse and control from the rider because the horse's back position, his bascule, becomes exaggerated.

Riding Vocab

Bascule is the position of the horse as he goes over a jump. The ideal position has the horse stretching out his neck and arching his back. The neck of most horses needs to be lower than their withers for them to get the distance or extension needed for good jumping.

Some jumps require the horse to clear more than one set of rails when he leaps. Usually, there is only an empty space between the jumps, but in a table jump, the space between the different hurdles is filled in. That part is the table. It has to be strong enough to hold the horse's weight, since many times, a horse will actually land on it, even though he is supposed to clear it.

Oxer Jumps

When an obstacle has more than one set of bars to clear, it is known as an oxer jump. The bars can be set in most any fashion, including parallel, ascending, descending, or hogsback, which is a set of three jumps with the one in the middle being the highest. A combination jump with three sets is called a triple bar and is the most difficult of the oxer jumps.

Water Jumps

A number of obstacles on a course contain water. A horse needs enough speed to clear a water jump but not too much to lose the rider. The length of the water can vary, but even at the highest levels of competition, the depth of the water is not to exceed 14 inches.

There are many types of combination jumps involving water. One of these is called a Trakehner, named after a breed from Eastern Europe. A Trakehner is a jump over a ditch, with rails set up in front of the water. The height of the rails varies depending on the level of competition.

Riding Vocab

A Trakehner jump got its name in the eighteenth century in Prussia. The King began a program that drained much of the very wet grounds of the country. This created a high number of drainage ditches. Afterward, the horses of the region were trained to leap over the ditches. Their ability to do so was one of the determining factors in deciding whether a horse was suitable for use in combat.

A horse may have to clear a fence to land in water and then may have to move through the water for a stride or two before leaping back out. If the horse is paying too little attention to the fence while preoccupied with the water, he will not be focused enough to clear the jump.

Jumping Fundamentals

You need to be in the proper position in the saddle to be a successful jumping rider. To get the best leverage from the reins, the rider should not be holding his hands too far up toward the horse's head, or back behind the withers. They need to be more in the middle of his crest, or upper half of his neck.

It's necessary for the rider to loosen the reins, or release them when the horse is going over a jump. For beginning riders, a basic release is used in which the rider holds onto the horse's mane as he jumps.

There are other variations to the release depending on the size of the jump. A short release loosens the grip only after the horse lifts, not before as in the other releases. In another variation called a long release, the rider should have his arms almost completely extended with a minimum amount of restraint on the reins when the maximum amount of lift is required.

The rider should make sure his stirrups are adjusted properly. If the feet are not set correctly, the rider will be either too high or too low out of the saddle. He will not be able to push off with enough authority, and the horse will not get enough momentum for the jump.

The rider should be in the classic two-point position, with the knees angled just past 90 degrees. The rider's body should be elevated just enough to clear the horse's back so he can spring into the jump.

The best way to get a horse to generate power from his hindquarters—his impulsion—is to have him trained to respond to leg signals. The rider should not try to generate power for a jump by lifting and pushing forward with his seat. This is not only less effective, but may cause the rider or the horse to lose balance.

The rider needs to be at the right distance from the jump when the horse springs up for the jump. Even if the rider makes a jump successfully, he might lose too much time regaining speed if the horse loses too much momentum.

There is no universally correct distance to be before each jump. It always depends on the height and width of the obstacle as well as the firmness of the ground. That's in addition to the horse's jumping ability.

Cross-Country

Cross-country competition is a race over obstacles and varying terrain. It tests both the horse's speed and his jumping ability. Basically, the course is meant to represent the old English countryside, with obstacles that are made up of all the items you would expect to find on a trek through the woods. These include water, logs, ditches, and banks.

The race resembles the type of jumping races that Thoroughbreds compete in at racetracks, especially in the United Kingdom. The main difference is that the course is set up over the countryside, not around a race track oval.

The races are set at distances between 2¾ miles and 4 miles. There are anywhere from twenty-four to thirty-six obstacles.

History of the Event

Originally, the cross-country competition was much longer and much more involved. There was a segment over flat ground followed by another phase over jumps, then back to another run over a flat course.

The horses were then examined by doctors in the part of the race known as the vet box. The horses that were deemed fit were allowed to continue to the last phase of the cross-country race.

Most competitions have abandoned all these preliminary legs and have retained just the last phase, the cross-country race. However, there are still some cross-country events that utilize all the historic phases, though the leading competitors in the sport do not compete in these historic phases.

Of the various events that make up English riding, cross-country is considered the least formal. Riders are dressed more casually and the horses are allowed to run with various bits of safety equipment attached.

The Obstacles

Courses are designed to show the courage of the horse and his trust in the rider. The difficulty that horses have with seeing in certain lights can be utilized to create jumps where the horse has to trust his rider, since he can't see the landing and is jumping blind.

Each jump is numbered, and each number is color coded to indicate which horse and rider team is required to make the jump. There are also flags at each obstacle. A white flag is on the left and a red flag is on the right. If the red flag has a stripe on it, it means the jump is optional.

The difficulty of the jumps depends on the level of competition. There is a beginner course, an intermediate one, and an advanced level. Sometimes a race incorporates all levels of jumpers and includes some obstacles that lower-level competitors avoid.

The standard expectation of speed is one factor that changes according to the level. The course is set up so that the advanced participants are expected to travel at a slightly faster speed than the beginner. The barriers are also higher and the width of the ditches is much greater for the advanced horses and riders, more than 2 feet wider. The change in elevation for such jumps as a drop fence obstacle is also greater for the advanced class.

Over time, as horses and riders compete, they accumulate points, which will get them moved into higher classifications. Points are given depending on the level of competition, where the horse finished and the number of competitors in the event. There are extra points awarded to horses for every clean run that did not knock off an obstacle.

The first level of classification is beginner, followed by novice, training, preliminary, intermediate and finally, advanced. There are point thresholds a horse had to meet to step up to a higher ranking. The final level, advanced, requires at least 61 points.

Horse Sense

The condition of the course in a cross-country event varies according to the location. Usually, the course is set over uneven terrain, but some events may be in places where, because of the climate, the ground is flatter and drier.

Usually, the course designer sets obstacles only for the advanced riders over uneven and hilly grounds, saving the flat terrain for less-experienced riders and horses.

Race Preparation

Before a cross-country race, riders walk the course to take note of the obstacles and all other pertinent details. The rider memorizes the locations and difficulties of all the jumps, noting when he will need to pick up speed and how he needs to approach each jump. He also takes note of the footing around each obstacle, especially if there has been inclement weather.

In his walk-through, the rider also takes note of any unexpected distractions that might come up during the race. Since these events are held in open areas, not in enclosed courses, anything you might find wandering around a farm might make an unscheduled appearance.

Start of the Race

Each competitor starts the race at a separate time. There is no match racing in cross-country; horse and rider teams compete against the clock and the course. At the start, the timekeeper counts down the time for the rider, who must wait at the start box until his time is called. The horse begins from a standing start and cannot be in motion to begin the race.

The early part of the course is not as difficult as the later part. The idea of most designers is to let the horse and rider build up their confidence before they encounter the more difficult sections of the course, which usually begin in the middle of the race. Near the end, the jumps tend to get a bit easier again. The course usually ends with the horse at a full gallop crossing the finish line.

Scoring

In an ideal ride, the horse's final time is his final score. But there are many penalties imposed for a number of different faults.

➤ There is a time penalty of 0.4 points for every second the horse exceeds the time limit. There is also a penalty for going too fast of 0.4 seconds over the limited time.

➤ Refusing to attempt a jump is penalized 20 points. A second refusal is penalized 40 points. If a horse has a third refusal at a jump, he is eliminated from the competition.

➤ Several actions result in immediate disqualification from an event as well as other possible disciplinary actions. These include willful obstruction of a competitor, failure to stop when signaled or attempting a jump when the rider has lost his helmet. Other grounds for immediate elimination include omission of an obstacle or jumping it in the wrong direction. If the rider or horse falls, the horse is also disqualified.

The Horses

Most of the horses competing in cross-country events are either Thoroughbreds or descendants of Thoroughbreds. They are the breed that best combines stamina with speed and endurance. Steeplechasing and hurdle races are a major part of Thoroughbred racing, at least in England and Ireland.

Riding Vocab

Steeplechasing is a race over hurdles and obstacles that originated in the English and Irish countrysides. The event got its name because the races usually had their finish line near a church, so the competitors would be riding in the direction of a high church steeple.

Hunt Seat

The history of English riding is quite evident in the competitions known as hunt seat. In the nineteenth century, English riders would head out to the countryside to hunt foxes or deer. They would follow a pack of dogs on the scent, and their horses would have to keep up with the chase over uneven ground while jumping fences, brooks, and natural impediments like fallen trees.

Hunt seat competitions are set up to resemble such activities, with the rider showing how well he can control his horse while the horse displays his ability to run and jump.

The horses in hunt seat competition are known as hunters or jumpers. They need to have the speed to run on level ground and the power to leap over obstacles, sometimes close to the height of the horse. Hunt seat events are sometimes called forward seat competitions.

Competitions

Hunt seat events are divided into several levels, or classes. There are events restricted by breeds, including a large category for pony hunters. There are three divisions for pony hunters (small, medium, and large), with the fences ranging from 26 inches up to 3 feet. Ponies that are green, or just starting, jump fences as low as just 24 inches high.

Green hunter classes for full-sized horses are divided into several levels. The fences for these horses are also shorter, below the standard 4 feet in height. There are also divisions for more experienced hunters that just can't jump as high.

Hunter competitions are also divided by the experience and age of the riders. The most basic distinction divides the riders between professionals and amateurs.

There are not only designated ages for children but for adults as well. Some hunt seat organizations offer a senior group for riders over fifty.

Not all horses in hunt seat competitions are jumpers. There are divisions strictly for flat ground competition.

Appearances

The horses and riders in hunt seat competitions both have a certain appearance. The horses' tails and manes are always braided so that they look neat for the events. Other hair on the horses' bodies is neatly trimmed and cleaned.

The riders wear the typical English riding shirt, jacket, and breeches. Usually, they do not wear a black coat, since that is considered the color for dressage competitions. Quite often, the coat is green, the darker shade known as hunter green.

Tack

Classical English riding tack is the norm for hunt seat competition, with a snaffle bridle and bit. The various types of snaffle bits are all used, including the D-ring and the eggbutt.

Some attachments are not allowed, including any kind of martingale to control the height of the horse's head.

Hunt Seat Saddles

A couple of different saddles are used in hunt seat and other English riding disciplines. These include the all-purpose saddle, which is also known as an eventing saddle, and a general-purpose saddle, which can be used for several different purposes, including dressage, cross-country riding, and jumping.

The all-purpose saddle includes a knee roll, which is a smoothed-down area of the saddle in the pad below the front of the seat. It is where the rider's knee goes when he's lifted forward by a jump. The knee roll makes it easier to slide, or roll, back into the saddle.

The all-purpose saddle is generally considered a beginner's saddle because it has a seat that is deep and safer than other English saddles. Advanced riders tend to find that the deep seat makes it difficult to obtain the proper position, especially those deep-seat saddles required for competitions.

Riding Vocab

An all-purpose saddle is the same as an eventing saddle, but saddles labeled as eventing saddles are usually more expensive.

Also used in hunt seat competition is an English jumping saddle, which is also known as a forward seat saddle, and a close contact saddle. The jumping saddle flap has a groove in the center for the leg. This allows the stirrups to be set lower, which gives the rider more leverage to ride at higher speed while signaling for a jump.

Like the all-purpose saddle, most versions of the jumping saddle have a knee roll on the flap. They also have a lower seat with both the front and the back low. This design gives the rider a more secure seat during a jump.

The Hunters

The show hunters are judged on their deportment and their strides. The scoring of their competitions is subjective, with the judges looking at the form of the horse during his jumps as well as the willingness of his response to the rider's commands. There is no standardized scoring for the judges of show hunters to use. It is all up to their discretion.

The jumps on the course are not as difficult or as demanding as they are in the other hunt seat competitions. There are few combination jumps and no water jumps.

The Show Jumpers

Unlike the hunters, show jumpers are judged strictly on their ability on the course. There are usually more jumps on the course for the jumpers than there are for the hunters. Show jumpers are also expected to handle obstacles that are both higher and wider than they are for hunters. The combinations are also more complex. There are water jumps to clear, and the turns are more difficult to negotiate. Pelham bits that include both a snaffle and a curb design are legal in some competitions.

The show jumpers are judged on the speed with which they can complete an event and on their ability to accumulate as few jumping faults as possible. There are 4 faults added to the horse's score for every rail knocked off and 4 faults for every jump refused. There is also a time limit for finishing the course. If the horse does not finish in the prescribed time, ¼ fault is added for each second beyond the limit.

The time limit adds a real test to the show jumper competition. It requires the horse and rider to move at a fairly rapid speed, but still be under enough control to set and have the proper footwork for each jump.

Show jumper competitions often offer a jump-off among all competitors who had a fault-free first round. There is usually a second, shorter course set up for the jump off. The fastest time in that phase of the event wins the jumper competition.

Equitation

Equitation judges the riders on their ability to get the horse to move while maintaining proper form and appearance in the saddle. Like show hunters, equitation scoring is subjective, with the judges examining the skill and control of the rider. The scoring is based just on the skill of the rider, not on the moves or form of the horse.

Hunt seat equitation is quite similar to western equitation (see Chapter 14) other than the variations of the movements. Sometimes, the riders not only go through a jumping course, but are also asked to perform certain tests. These include making the horse halt, switch strides, back up, or ride in a circle. In some equitation events, no jumps are used. All of the competitions are over flat ground.

The courses for hunt seat equitation are somewhat similar to the ones faced by hunters, but they are usually more difficult. They have tighter turns and there are more combinations for the horse and rider to negotiate.

Hunt seat equitation is usually considered an activity for young riders. It is considered to be a competition that helps develop young riders into expert riders in hunter or jumper competitions.

Eventing

Eventing is sort of the equine equivalent of the decathlon, as horses compete in three different disciplines. The event takes place over three days, with a dressage competition to begin, followed by a cross-country race before the final day, which is show jumping inside a ring.

CHAPTER 17

 # Polo

---

In This Chapter

➤ History and fundamentals of the sport

➤ The polo pony

➤ How to get involved in the sport

In this chapter, you'll learn about the ancient game of polo, one of the most enjoyable and vigorous equine activities. You'll learn about the history of the game, which goes back well over 1,000 years, and how polo is now played throughout the world. You'll learn about the polo ponies, which really aren't ponies. And you'll learn how you can get involved in the game and what the expenses are likely to be.

History of the Game

Polo is an ancient sport that was played in Persia at least fifteen centuries ago but perhaps as long ago as twenty centuries. Originally, it was devised as a form of practice for combat. The dozens of players on each team were made up of soldiers from the Persian cavalry.

As the sport evolved, it became known as the sport of kings, since it was played by the nobility, both men and women. But even when the popularity of the game spread from Persia into India and China, it was still considered a good game for training soldiers on horseback.

Riding Vocab

Polo is known as the sport of kings because it was the game played by the rulers of Persia and other countries that had adopted it. But in more recent times, the sport of horse racing has also been known, especially in England, as the sport of kings. The name was given not because the royalty were participants in races, but because they owned and bred the horses. This moniker continues into the modern era through Queen Elizabeth II, a horse owner and breeder, and her mother, who was also a Thoroughbred racing enthusiast.

The Modern Game

Polo as we know it today is derived from the game as it was played in India early in the nineteenth century. From there, the ruling British took up the game and formed polo clubs. With the empire in full force and scope, the British spread the game to many other regions of the world, in particular, North and South America.

The Indian form of the game had seven players on a side, and there were actual ponies used to play the game, usually about 13 hands in height. The field was about 225 yards in length, shorter than the current size.

Riding Vocab

The word polo is derived from an old Tibetan word, pulu, which means "ball."

The playing surface in polo is referred to as the pitch.

The word chukka is derived from a Hindi word, cakkar, which means "circle" or "wheel."

Rules of the Game

Polo is fairly similar to many other sports, such as field hockey, lacrosse, and even croquet. The difference is it is played on horseback. By comparison with other outdoor sports, the polo field is quite large, stretching out for 300 yards with a width of 160 yards. It is three time longer than a football field and almost three times as wide. Of course, this is necessary because of the speed of the horses and the room they need to maneuver.

The object of the game is to get the ball between the goal posts, which are centered on the goal lines at each end of the field. Players move a hard plastic ball forward with a mallet that is 51 inches long. All contact with the mallet must be made from the right side. Players must be adept enough to swing the mallet while holding the reins and holding (and occasionally using) a whip.

The only times the action in polo is stopped is if a horse and rider have equipment trouble, there is an injury, or a penalty is called.

The sport is divided into periods, known as chukkas, sometimes spelled chukkers. There can be anywhere from four to eight chukkas that make up a polo match, depending on the level of competition and the quality and availability of polo ponies. Each chukka is seven minutes long, which was considered the longest amount of time that a horse could exert himself before needing a rest. Normally in modern polo, a new polo pony is used by each player for each chukka.

The periods are supposed to be seven minutes long, but after the elapsed time, if there is no stoppage in play, the game continues on for another half minute. There are four minutes between chukkas as well as a halftime that goes on for ten minutes.

During halftime, spectators are allowed on the field to take part in divot stomping. This helps repair the ground that was torn up by several tons of horses and riders. Divot stomping is traditionally considered a time for spectators to get to know each other, sort of like a church social. But, of course, having the spectators repairing divots is an inexpensive way to repair the ground.

Horse Sense

The famous stadium in New York called the Polo Grounds was the home of polo when it first opened in 1876. Polo was played there until 1880.

After that, the stadium and three subsequent parks in the same area were all known as the Polo Grounds even though no polo was played there. In 1963, the last of the four parks with that name, which had been built in 1911, was finally closed and demolished.

However, not far away in Long Island, a large and famous polo field, Meadowbrook Farm, was opened in 1881. It has been the site for many famous polo matches through the years. It is still in operation today.

Penalties

Because of the dangers inherent in a sport with eight horses running around the field at high speed, the rules are designed primarily for safety. The main rule of the game is called line of the ball. It gives the player who is controlling the ball the right of way on the field. Any attempt to impede his progress by cutting in front of him is a foul.

Even so, there are some risky moves that are allowed on the field. These are moves that come from the side, which is considered okay. In order to take the ball away, another player can actually use his own horse to bump into the shoulder or hip of the horse of an opponent. The term for this is riding off.

A player can also try to hook the mallet of the opponent controlling the ball. If all else fails, the player can just reach in with his own mallet and knock the ball away.

In addition to staying clear of the other player's path, each rider is also prohibited from touching another player with the mallet or bumping into him or his horse with his body.

The Umpires

The game is run by two umpires who move about the field on horseback. When a foul is called, both umpires must agree on the call. If there is a dispute, a third man, the referee, is called in. This official sits on the center line during the action. The third man's decision is final.

Not only can the officials call fouls and designated penalties, they can also impose fines on players for serious breaches of the rules and recommend further disciplinary action.

The Flagmen

Each of the two flagmen is positioned on opposite goal lines and give a signal if a goal has been scored. They also give a signal if the ball has crossed the goal line without a goal being scored. When that happens, the flagman puts the ball at the spot where it crossed the goal line, so a player on the other team can put it back into play. Putting the ball back onto the field is called a knock in.

Whatever ruling the flagmen may make can be overruled by the umpires as well as the referee.

The Players

The rules of participating groups or organizations determine age limits and gender restrictions on the team, if any. There are four players on each of the two teams. Each one of the four players on a team has a number, which is clearly visible on their shirts, and a designated assignment:

> ➤ Player 1: Positioned to be the most offensive-minded player
> ➤ Player 2: The next in line after player 1 moving toward the goal
> ➤ Player 3: Positioned in the middle of the field as the playmaker on the team; often considered the best player on the field, though sometimes player 2 may also get that designation
> ➤ Player 4: Play a strictly defensive position

Handicaps

Handicapping the players is a system that has been in place in the sport for over a century. It was a system devised to make the competition of two teams competitive, even if the players were of different levels.

The handicap rankings take several factors into consideration:

> ➤ The quality of a player's riding skill
> ➤ The quality of a player's horse
> ➤ A player's apparent knowledge of the game, including use of strategy, level of team play, and level of sportsmanship

A handicap is not specifically a listing of the number of goals that a player is expected to score in a match, but it is an indication of his worth to the team. The handicap ratings start at -2 for players who are complete novices and go up to 10, which is the rating for the best players in the world. Very few players in the world are given a 10 handicap. Most players are given handicaps somewhere around 2 or 3. It's rare for anyone but a professional to get a handicap score of 5 or higher.

The handicaps are added up for all four players on each team. The discrepancy between the two teams is put into the score to start the game. So if team A has a handicap total of 5 and team B has a total of 3, team B begins the game with a 2-goal advantage.

Handicaps are not a factor in the open competitions among the world's best players, but all players are given rankings, anyway.

Polo Variations

Though the game is best known for play on a big outdoor field, an indoor version of the sport is also popular. It's called arena polo. It's played indoors on a much smaller field. The standard size of the arena is 100 yards long and 50 wide, but many arenas aren't that big. The minimum size is 50 × 25 yards.

Horse Sense

The advantage to playing indoors is the year-round availability of the game. While your regular summer polo field might be covered in several inches of snow, the indoor arena is conceivably always available.

The indoor surface is made of dirt and sand, not the grass fields of the outdoor game. There are only three players on a team in arena games. The fourth player is eliminated because of the smaller area of play.

Arena polo uses a different ball than the outdoor version. It's not as hard but it's bigger—much bigger in size, if not in weight. It is at least 12 inches around and may be as big as 15 inches around. No matter the size, it weighs only slightly more than the outdoor ball. Another difference is that the arena polo ball is inflatable rather than hard plastic. Goal sizes are usually the same as the outdoor game, though that can vary depending on the sponsoring club or organization.

Since the horses and riders in the arena game do not have as much room to maneuver, the game is not as fast and there is more contact among the players than there is with the outdoor sport.

The Equipment

The path to becoming a good player in polo requires a mastering of the equipment. It is not easy to stay balanced on a horse and carry several items in your hands at the same time, let alone have to reach over the side with your polo stick to swat a ball. But this is all required to become a decent player in the sport.

Much of the equipment for polo is strictly for safety, as the game can be quite dangerous. Not only is it played at a rapid pace, but hard objects are being swung about, and there is contact among the horses.

Balls and Mallets

In the past, the polo ball was made of natural material, usually hard plant matter such as bamboo. Today, it is made of plastic. It is a little over 3 inches in diameter and weighs about a ¼ pound.

The standard length of a mallet is 51 inches. It can be an inch or two shorter or longer depending on the size of the horse and the length of the rider's arms.

The shaft of a mallet is made of hard cane, the most popular of which comes from a palm called manau. It grows in the jungles of Asia and can grow to heights of 600 feet in just fifteen years. The cut manau cane is boiled in coconut oil for fifteen minutes, cleaned in sand and water, and then stacked to dry. The product eventually becomes beige and gold.

Riding Vocab

The term mallet is used only in the United States. In England, this piece of polo equipment is known as a polo stick.

The polo mallet looks quite a bit like a number of putters you might have in your golf bag. Of course, that's not surprising because the basic purpose is similar.

The head at the end of the shaft is straight and normally 9 inches long. It is made from a durable South American wood called tipa.

The top of the mallet has a grip made of rubber. It usually contains a webbed thong for the thumb.

The Polo Saddle

The saddle used to ride in polo matches is an English saddle. There's no horn or any of the other western saddle features. The seat is not deep, and is instead designed to give the rider ease of movement when swinging his arm to hit the ball with his mallet.

The saddle flaps have a long and wide design to protect the horse from the rider's frequent leg moves.

Though the saddle is considered English, at least some features of the stirrups are perhaps more reminiscent of those on a western saddle. The irons themselves are heavy, and the leathers are wide and thick, something not seen on a dressage or eventing saddle. This provides extra safety for the rider and the horse as they deal with the frequent contact in the sport.

Horses are also often equipped with a breastplate at the front of the saddle, which allows for the attachment of a martingale or a tie down. Those pieces aid the rider in keeping the horse's head from getting too high.

Polo Bridles

The bridles worn by polo ponies are usually snaffle bridles with a browband and noseband, among other parts. Frequently a pelham double bridle is used, containing both a snaffle bit and a curb bit.

Having both types of bits gives the rider more choices for directing his horse. Considering the rider is also holding a mallet and a whip in his hand, there is a lot of skill needed to control those items as well as the two reins that each control one type of bit.

Leg Pads and Other Safety Measures

In addition to all the equipment the horse is wearing, there are some other safety measures taken to help protect the horses. The horse's front and back cannon bones are taped to protect their legs against injury from direct contact with a mallet. And usually the mane is shaved down and the tail is braided to prevent the horse's hair from getting tangled in a mallet.

The Rider's Equipment

Polo is a contact sport, at least from the thighs down, so the rider needs to wear a good deal of protective equipment, such as the following:

➤ Thick boots for protection; they must be a dark color, either black or brown

➤ Spurs attached to their boots to help signal their horses

➤ White pants worn tucked into boots

➤ Dark-colored knee pads

➤ Polo helmet with specific requirements for the sport

➤ Face guard resembling the single-bar face mask of a football helmet

➤ Protective goggles that are stronger than those worn by most riders because they need to withstand the possible contact they may receive from a swinging mallet or a flying ball

➤ Protective gloves

Polo Ponies

Ponies were the equines that were used in India during the nineteenth century when the game was first recognized and adapted in the West. In the Manipur region, the game was played on Manipuri ponies, which stood at 13 hands or less. But ponies are no longer seen on the field. The game is played with full-sized horses from 14 to 16 hands. The term polo pony, however, is still in use, possibly because of its pleasant-sounding alliteration.

Many of the polo ponies in use today are Thoroughbreds or descended from Thoroughbreds, because of their speed, stamina, and agility. But good polo horses can come from any background. Many have been found working on ranches.

The best polo ponies are bred in Argentina, where the world's best players currently compete. The ponies can be traced back to the criollo, one of many breeds brought to the Americas by the Spanish conquistadores. It is still a popular horse throughout Latin America. The breed is noted for its toughness, stamina, and endurance.

Criollo mares were crossed with Thoroughbred stallions, which produced outstanding polo ponies that combine the best qualities of both its ancestors. They have the speed and agility of the Thoroughbred with the toughness of the criollo.

In North America, many of the most successful polo horses have come by crossing Thoroughbreds with quarter horses. The best of this cross have the quick bursts of speed of the quarter horse combined with the greater power and stamina of the Thoroughbred.

Equine Tip

You can't just show up on the polo field with your horse and expect him to know what to do and how to react. It takes at least six months of training before a horse can be used as a polo pony, though sometimes it can take longer than that, even years, before a horse is considered ready for competition.

Training a Polo Pony

It's rare for polo ponies to be trained before they reach the age of three. They usually reach their peak somewhere around the age of six. They can keep being used in the sport for a long time, often until they are twenty years old.

In the sport of polo, having the best polo ponies on your team is considered at least as important as having the best players.

Professional Polo

There are professional polo teams throughout South America as well as in many other countries where the sport is popular. It's not unusual for the owner of a team to also be one of the players.

The owner of the team pays the players, provides living facilities for them and their families, and also buys and cares for the polo ponies. Expenses to run a polo team usually run about $1 million a year.

The top polo players are usually paid a salary, ranging from about $50,000 a year on up to $500,000 and even more.

World Championships

Polo was an Olympic sport until World War II. Since then, an international body began a polo world championship tournament, something along the lines of soccer's World Cup. But there is a rule that limits the handicaps of the four-man teams to 14, which keeps all the world's top players out of the competition.

The championships are held every three or four years in many locations around the world, much like the Olympics. Since most of the top players in the world have long been thought to come from South America, it's not surprising that through 2011, Argentina has won four championships, Brazil three, and Chile one. Only one other country has won a championship, the United States in 1989.

Playing Polo

You've become a fan of polo and you want to become a participant in the sport. First, you'll need to learn how to play the game.

Getting Involved

The normal path to becoming a polo player requires you first to get a horse—actually a string of horses—for the sport. This of course is expensive. A top horse that can compete at the top levels of the sport can sell for $50,000 or even more. But you can find a useful horse for somewhere around $10,000 to $15,000. You will likely need at least four horses, but more likely seven or eight if you are going to be a competitive player in the sport.

Riding Vocab

While there are not an official ranking for horses as there are for players, the people in the sport divide the quality of polo ponies into three categories:

1. High goal: The best horses

2. Medium goal: The average horses

3. Low goal: The lower quality horses

The pricing of horses is based on which of the three categories the pony is listed. Low-goal ponies can be bought for as little as $5,000, even if they are sound, whereas high-goal ponies are worth at least $30,000, though some can be worth even more.

The horses are just part of the usual expenses required for the sport. A helmet will cost you anywhere from $250 to $400. Polo boots, with their extra padding, are quite expensive, usually starting at $400 but going up to close to $1,000.

There are also knee guards, which cost from $200 to $300. Your riding pants and shirts will cost about $100 combined.

Then there are the expenses for equipment you won't be wearing. The cost of a polo saddle is about the same as other saddles, ranging from $750 to well over $1,000. The bridles for polo are about $250, and the wraps to go around your polo pony's legs are about $100.

Don't forget to budget for the cost of a mallet, which is about another $500.

These costs are in addition to the other everyday expenses that horse ownership entails, such as stabling, feeding, caring for, and keeping the horse healthy through veterinary visits.

Cheaper Ways to Get Involved

If you're able to afford the expense of getting training and owning and caring for a string of horses, fine. Go to it. But you don't have to have all those costs to get involved in the sport.

Learning to Ride and Learning to Play Polo

You can't just go to the local sporting goods store to buy some equipment and start playing the game. You'll need to go to a training center and take lessons to learn the sport.

You don't have to know how to ride a horse before you learn polo. You can learn to do both at the same time. You don't have to go to a riding academy for your first riding experiences. A polo training center will teach you all you need to know to ride and also teach you how to play the game.

Finding a Polo Club

There are polo clubs in virtually all areas of the country. There are more than twenty clubs in New York State and about thirty in California. They are all sanctioned and working with the governing body of the sport in the country, the United States Polo Association (USPA). In the United States, there is also a group that handles polo events just for women, the United States Women's Polo Association (USWPA).

Eventually, you can join a club and rent ponies to play the sport as frequently as every weekend. You can also rent all the necessary equipment.

In an attempt to expand interest and participation, polo organizations have tried hard to make it more affordable to play polo. Taking part in the sport no longer requires the possibly overwhelming expense of owning your own stable of horses.

Polo organizations have also had an eye on the future of the sport by creating youth groups throughout the country. This part of the USPA provides an introduction to as well as lessons in the sport for young people. Lessons in polo usually are offered for children age ten and up.

PART FIVE

A Horse of Your Own

CHAPTER 18

Buying a Horse

> ## In This Chapter
>
> ➤ Considerations and advice
> ➤ Checking out your options
> ➤ The test drive
> ➤ Final decision

In this chapter, you'll learn what steps to take once you've decided to buy a horse and what your alternatives are. You'll learn what questions to ask and what to look for when you inspect a horse. You'll learn what to look for when you inspect the horse. And you'll discover what to look for when you test ride your prospective purchase.

The Pros and Cons of Horse Ownership

You've decided to buy a horse and you've decided what kind of horse you want. Now you're ready to make your purchase. You're excited to have a horse of your own, one that you and maybe many members of your family can ride.

The Pros

If you have young children or grandchildren, the excitement of watching them get on the horse you choose and learn to ride will be exciting for you, and will result in stronger bonds between you and your family members.

As an owner, there's no more waiting for a horse at a stable to become available for you. You're also not restricted to ride on a particular day of the week or at a particular time of day. The extra conveniences of owning a horse are many.

The Cons

There are certainly great pleasures in owning a horse, but there are problems, too. You may enjoy riding a horse you've rented for the afternoon. But owning a horse is a much bigger responsibility. It's a bit like going from being a babysitter to being a parent. Suddenly, all the problems, as well as the expenses, of the horse are yours.

Before you decide to take the big step of purchasing a horse, make sure you can handle the expenses. You not only have to feed the horse, you have to pay for his vet bills, his shoeing, and his equipment. You also have to pay for his boarding and all the extra costs that boarding entails.

If you have your own place to keep your horse, be it a farm or some other large area, there are still costs for caring for his stall, keeping it ventilated, and keeping the paths clean. You might also need to hire a caretaker to look after your horse. These added expenses can run into the thousands of dollars.

Just make sure you've considered all the expenses you'll have in addition to the actual purchase price of a horse. It would be a bad deal in many ways if you bought a horse and found out not long after that you simply can't keep up with the expenses.

Getting Good Advice

The first person to talk to about purchasing a horse is your trainer, someone knowledgeable who you can trust. Tell him why you want to buy a horse and how much you want to spend. Listen to what he has to say. He might recommend that you don't buy a horse just yet and lease one instead.

After your discussion, if the final decision is for you to go ahead and buy a horse, have him advise you where to purchase one. He can tell you what kind of horse is right for you and where you can find one.

The accepted practice in the horse industry is that if you consult a trainer or some other professional in the business to find a horse, you should pay them either a negotiated fee or 10 percent of your purchase price.

Options for Getting a Horse

Buying a horse from an owner isn't your only option. For a lot less money, you could adopt a homeless horse from a reputable organization. Or, just as with cars, you don't have to buy a horse—you can lease one.

The Leasing Alternative

Just as with cars, you don't have to buy a horse, you can lease one. The horse-leasing business is not nearly as established as the auto-leasing business, so it's harder to find a horse to lease. But the principles are the same—you take control of the property for a certain time, pay all the expenses, and then return the item, in this case the horse, at the end of the designated time period.

Leasing a horse is a good initial alternative to owning your first horse, since it will let you see if it's what you want without the full expenses or obligations of owning.

The person leasing the horse does not have the option of selling the horse to recoup his expenses, but he also doesn't have the risk of losing all value if something happens to the horse.

The costs for a lease can vary. One lease agreement is to pay a certain percentage of the horse's value to the owner, usually about 25 percent, in exchange for the use of the horse. There are other lease arrangements, including sharing a lease with someone else. Since a horse for riding isn't really like a car and you don't need access to him all the time, this might be the best alternative for a prospective first-time owner. A shared horse lease will keep the expenses down and probably won't much reduce your riding time, if at all.

Generally, horses for lease are not as easy to find as horses for sale, but if you ask the various horse people you encounter, they should be able to alert you to any opportunities.

Horse Adoptions and Rescues

If you're looking to acquire a horse but don't know where to find one, you might well consider adopting a horse. Virtually every area of the country has an organization that helps find homes for horses that don't have one. Many of the groups that have worked with other animals in need of homes, such as dogs and cats, also work with horses. Such organizations as Rescue Me and RescueShelter.com have horses that are up for adoption at a reasonable cost.

Many of these horses are still quite useful but may have been abandoned by an owner for financial reasons. Some are old racehorses that have outlived their usefulness on the track.

Most of the horses available in these services have no temperamental problems and are reasonably sound. The purchase price for them is usually under $1,000, sometimes well under.

Even if you don't adopt a horse through one of these adoption and rescue services, you should certainly consider a donation for the humane work that they provide.

Horse Sense

It might be a surprise to learn that horses that were in the wild usually adapt well once they are taken in by caring owners. One owner who adapted several mustangs said the horses behaved fine once they figured out that they weren't going to be eaten.

For the most part, formerly wild horses just need love and kindness before they adapt to a domestic setting.

There are other adoptions offered by the Bureau of Land Management (BLM). These adoptions offer horses that were taken from lands that do not have enough food to support them. Rather than just slaughter them, attempts are made to find homes for them. The Wild Horse and Burro Program is based primarily in the West, though there is a pickup facility as far east as West Virginia.

The BLM has auctions, usually every few months, on the Internet. You must register in advance and show the BLM that you have adequate facilities to house and care for the horse. Deposits are required before you can bid on a horse. Opening bids must be no lower than $125, than can be increased by as little as $5 until the horse is sold.

If you have made a successful bid, you can arrange for a pickup from a holding center. You must have a proper trailer to transport the horse. You can also decline the horse at that point if there is some problem you didn't previously detect. Returning the horse gives you a credit toward a future adoption.

There have been many questions raised about the humane treatment of the horses and other animals in the BLM replacement program. There are also issues about the way the animals are captured and the conditions in which they are kept. It's up to you whether these disturbing reports make you reluctant to become involved with the Bureau of Land Management program, or if they give you a greater urge to rescue one of these animals.

Even if you don't adopt a horse through one of these adoption and rescue services, you should certainly consider a donation for the humane work that they provide.

Buying Your Horse

Remember that buying a horse isn't much different from buying a car, except that unless you're breeding your own stock, all the horses for sale are used. There can be as many problems with horses as there can be with previously owned cars.

Check the Internet closely to try to find a good price. Also, go to chat rooms and other forums where your questions about buying a horse can be answered. You might find out more information about certain breeds that you didn't know, and you might find out things about certain people selling horses that are of interest.

Checking Out the Horses

Once you've found what you think is a reputable farm or individual who can sell you a horse, you're ready to check out the prospects. Make the calls to arrange for an inspection of the horse you might be buying.

When you get there, obviously, you'll want to look at the horse closely. No matter how much you're going to spend on a horse, it's going to be a major investment, not just for the immediate sale price, but for the expenses to come. The healthier the horse is, the less you'll have to pay in the future for veterinarian bills or extra equipment.

Initial Questions

When you talk to a potential seller, the first thing you'll want to know is why the horse is for sale. Of course, you may not get a legitimate answer. If the horse is being sold because he's always hurt or has a terrible disposition, you probably won't hear about it. But ask the question anyway.

Chances are new horses are coming into the stable or the seller has too many horses. At least the seller will tell you something like that. If there's some negative reason that the horse is being sold and the seller does tell you so, you might respect his honesty but may not want his horse.

Find out the horse's age. There are advantages to older horses, since they might be calmer and easier to handle. But they probably also have more physical ailments.

Once the horse is out of the stall, you'll want to look back in the stall for any signs of trouble. See if there are signs that the horse frequently kicks the stall, which is an indication of temperament problems. Also, see if he's been chewing the wood around the stall. This is not necessarily a deal breaker for most horse purchases, but if this is your first purchase, you really don't need to deal with a horse that has that habit.

Watch how the horse moves about. He should look spry with good motion.

Riding Vocab

A horse that chews the wood around his stall is called a cribber. At horse auctions, it's disclosed if a horse has this trait.

Some areas of the world worry more about cribbers than others. Horsemen from Europe tend to want nothing to do with such horses. During the 1970s, two highly sought-after Thoroughbred stallion prospects, Icecapade and Halo, were originally sold to breeding farms in Europe but were returned after they were determined to be cribbers. Both returned to the United States, where they proceeded to have very successful, productive, and lengthy careers at stud.

The Prospect's Conformation

Look over the horse closely. You don't want a horse with physical flaws. Check out his legs. Make sure he has no glaring problem, such as cow hocks, when the knees on the hind legs are set too close together, or sickle hocks, where the hind ankles are set at too sharp an angle. You also don't want his front legs to be over at the knee. This will put too much pressure on his legs right away.

Look for signs of wear. Check his legs for scars and his back and sides for saddle sores.

Also check for signs of pin firing. This is a controversial type of treatment for injuries in the legs, mostly in the cannon bones. Extreme heat is applied to the injury to speed the healing process. It is not often practiced today. It involves the use of heated chemicals that leaves a mark on the horse.

The best idea is to stay away from horses that have received this treatment. Not only is it a sign of a past injury, but it also means that the treatment was given in lieu of giving the horse the proper time to heal from an injury, which might well have created other problems you can't see.

Next, you'll want to inspect all the hooves. You're not going to be able to ride the horse if he has problems with his feet. Smell the horse's feet for any unpleasant odors. Then clean off the hooves to inspect them. Look for any cracks or chips, and make sure the lines separating the parts of the hoof are correct.

One last sign to look for on the horse's feet is the type of shoe he is wearing. You don't want a horse that needs special protective shoes, which are obviously a sign of problems.

Next, check the teeth. There are a lot of old sayings around about buying a horse. The most famous might be, "Don't look a gift horse in the mouth." If the horse was given to you, you might well find something in his mouth that explains why. Damaged teeth or gums are a bad sign. At the very least, they will cost you a lot of money to fix. While you're looking in the horse's mouth, also check for missing teeth.

If the horse has passed your physical exam, you should also get the opinion of those with more knowledge than you. Have an experienced horsemen look over the horse as well. At this point, you also might want to schedule an examination by a veterinarian, though, because of the expenses of it, you probably should wait on that until you've made your final decision.

Equine Tip

Make sure the horse you pick out is appropriate for the environment you live in. If you're planning to ride your horse over mountainous terrain, make sure he is strong enough to hold you or whoever else will be riding him. You might find a smaller pony adorable, but that's not a reason to buy him if he can't carry your weight up the hills that you want to ride.

More Questions

If you are satisfied with the horse's condition, there are still questions to ask the seller. Find out about the horse's history. If he's a Thoroughbred or quarter horse, for instance, find out if he was ever used for racing.

You'll also want to know how much and what type of riding the horse has experienced. If you have relatives, such as children or grandchildren, that will be riding your horse, find out if the horse is good with children.

Another question to ask is about the horse's bloodlines. Is he a member of a registered breed, and, if so, does he have papers? This needn't be the deciding factor when picking out a horse. You can be perfectly happy with a mixed breed, known as a grade horse, if he's in good health and is a joy to ride. But if he is a registered breed, you'd like to have his papers, which might help your resale price if you should ever decide to sell him.

The Next Step

Now that you've looked over several horses, and you've decided which horse you want to buy, you need to follow the next step and start working with the horse directly.

Get up close with the horse and find out if he's affectionate to you. Perhaps you like the horse, but for some reason, he doesn't like you. Maybe give it a little time. This will be a big move for both of you.

Next, you'll want to try to tack up your horse. If he becomes your horse, you'll want to, or need to, be able to put the saddle on him, not to mention all the other gear. Find out if you can do this comfortably without the horse objecting to your personal way of putting on the equipment.

Another insight before you make your decision will be to examine the bit you're given as part of his equipment. Is it the type of bit you like to ride with, or is it a severe bit that indicates an uncooperative horse?

If you're able to get the tack on the horse without a problem, it's time to get on him. See if you two are able to move around nicely. See how well he responds to your commands. Make sure he moves in a fluent manner.

Begin by getting the horse to start walking. Then make sure you can get him to stop easily. Then get him to turn a few times. Then get him to go through his stride progressions. Go from the walk to the trot and to the canter, but don't let him gallop until you're in a safe place and you know you have control of him. Never let a new horse gallop until you're sure you have control of him while he's cantering.

At this point, you should make a preliminary appraisal of your prospective purchase. Take note of any problems he gave you. Did he respond well to your instructions? How comfortable do you feel on his back, and how happy are you with the way he's moving?

This might be enough riding for your introduction to the horse and if everything is still a go, you'll want to arrange to ride the horse at least once more before buying him.

The next time, you'll want to get even more answers. You need to perform whatever activity you want to take part in with your horse. If you want him to be a jumper, you should go over some hurdles. If you're looking for a horse to ride out on trails, you need to take him there to see how he'll respond.

See how the horse responds to different situations. Make sure he's not easily spooked by things he's likely to encounter with you if you buy him. He shouldn't be afraid of logs or other natural impediments that are lying about. You also don't want him getting too excited when he sees other creatures out on the trail, be they birds, squirrels, or other people.

If possible, while you're giving him what amounts to a test drive, see if you can get him around other horses. Make sure he interacts well with other horses and also with other people. See if he's a natural follower or leader. This will give you more insight into his personality.

At the end of the ride, you and your prospective horse should be getting along. Make sure the horse is not in too big a hurry to get back to the barn. That's not a good sign for several reasons, including the fact that he may want to get away from you as soon as possible.

The Final Decision

You've checked over all your options, you've had your "test drives," you've consulted with people who know more than you and you've talked it over with your family or friends. Once you've decided which horse you're going to buy,the last step is the final negotiation with the seller. If you can get an acceptable final price, you're probably quite excited and ready to make your purchase.

You're now the owner of a horse! Your next question is, what else do I need to do, and what else do I need to buy? If you haven't already decided where to board him, you also need to figure out where you're going to keep him.

CHAPTER 19

A New Owner's Guide

> ## In This Chapter
>
> ➤ Finding a location
>
> ➤ The equipment you'll need
>
> ➤ All about trailers

In this chapter, you'll learn what you need to do once you've purchased a horse. You'll learn how to pick out a location for your horse to be stabled and about all the equipment you'll need to buy. You'll also learn about trailering your horse.

Where to Keep Your Horse

The factors that go into deciding where to board your horse are similar to those that go into deciding where to take lessons. There is just more to it. You no longer have the goal of just finding a good, convenient, and professional place to ride. Now you're really involved and need a place to keep your own property. Some people feel more comfortable making this decision before they purchase their horse.

So go about the business of inspecting your options. Follow the same steps you did when you were looking for lessons. But since you're not just a person passing through the place for lessons, you need to know more about how the place is run. You want your horse to be safe and secure, so check out the following and decide if you like what you see:

➤ Where in the stable would you keep your equipment

➤ Look very closely at the tack room, which is where your own equipment would be stored

➤ Find out how and when your horse would be fed.

➤ Find out what the stable will provide and what you need to pay for

So go about the business of inspecting your options. Follow the same steps you did when you were looking for lessons.

If you purchased your horse from a stable or barn where you've already been riding, your choice of a barn is already made for you. Chances are you already came to an understanding of the new arrangement when you bought the horse.

Now that you own your own horse, you need to get your own equipment. You can see what equipment you can use at the stable where you're boarding your horse. But you'll have to and want to buy some of your own equipment.

Small Grooming Tools

Even if you're boarding your horse somewhere that provides grooming products, it's a good idea to buy your horse his own items. Brushes that are used on several horses can pick up germs or parasites that can easily be passed on.

➤ Soft brush: Used to gently rub the horse, even in delicate locations. Brushing with the soft bristles can help the horse's circulation as well as polish his coat. These brushes are soft enough that they can even be used on the face, around the eyes and nose. You can find different sizes of brushes that match the size of the area they are designed to be used.

➤ Hard brush: Designed for use when the horse has a longer coat. Since the bristles are hard, brushing can be painful for the horse if you're not careful. Any sensitive spots, including the stomach, shouldn't be treated with a hard brush.

➤ Shedding blade: Used to trim the horse's coat. It has a serrated edge and should not be used on any sensitive areas of the horse's body, meaning his head or his legs.

➤ Curry comb: A round comb with a lot of teeth that clears off the shedding hair while also giving the horse a bit of a rubdown. A curry comb is usually applied in a circular motion. There are several variations in curry combs, both in size and material.

➤ Grooming mitt: A large mitten that you use to rub the horse thoroughly. It is quite gentle and can be used on almost any part of the horse's body.

➤ Jelly scrubber: A small mitt with large bristles on one side and much smaller ones on the other. Some parts of the horse's body need the larger bristles of the scrubber, while his more sensitive parts will need the smoother side. The size you choose depends on the season and the length of the horse's coat.

➤ Hoof pick: An inexpensive item that can clean off the horse's hoof before dirt and other foreign particles can work their way into the foot.

Dressings and Shampoos

An important item to get for your horse is a hoof dressing, which is designed to keep the horse's hoof moist. There is always a danger of a hoof getting too dry, which can lead to painful and debilitating cracks in the wall.

Horse shampoos are also not that expensive, and are easily obtainable. There are shampoos that address the particular needs or problems of your horse's coat.

Blankets

Horses are wrapped with blankets to keep them warm or to keep them dry. Horses that are kept outside grow a thick coat that insulates them from the cold. But if your horse is kept indoors most of the day, he'll appreciate a blanket if he's outside and the temperature is below 50 degrees. Even if it's below 60 degrees, a blanket is a good idea if the horse has just had his coat clipped. The length of the horse's coat should also determine the heaviness of the blanket.

Though blankets can provide warmth in cold and keep your horse dryer in the rain, do not assume that they offer enough protection for either condition. Blankets are not designed to be long-term solutions to either problem. If a horse is left outside and has no shelter to protect him, a blanket will not keep him dry enough in a steady rain, nor will it keep him warm enough in very cold conditions.

Equine Tip

It's important that horses are not kept in a warm blanket when temperatures rise. Though almost all blankets are considered to be breathable, they cannot prevent the horse from overheating if the temperature rises too much.

Blankets are made of many materials, but canvas is the most common. There are also blankets made of fleece and others of nylon, which is waterproof.

More expensive blankets contain other materials, such as Teflon, which are used for water resistance.

Measuring for a Blanket

The blanket you buy your horse has to fit him. Measure your horse from the front of the chest to the middle of the hind legs. Sizes range from 68 inches to 84 inches. Blankets are rated for warmth, so be sure you get one that is best for your climate.

Attaching the Blanket

There are different styles of blankets with various ways to connect and wrap them. Some blankets have buckles that connect in the front. They may also contain Velcro, which helps hold them together.

A blanket that is connected and closed around the chest is called an open front blanket. It has flaps that stretch out in front of the horse's chest before they are fastened together.

Neck Rub Connectors are the D-rings in the blankets. They are on the part of the blanket that is placed near the withers. A hood or neck protector can be connected to them.

Belly straps hang below the blanket. There can be one, two, or three straps. They attach with either Velcro or buckles. If there are three, two of them are crossed when the blanket is tied to provide for extra strength.

There is also a belly band used on blankets, which is longer than the belly strap and much thicker. It pulls up over the sides onto the horse's back. It also can be attached with either a buckle or with Velcro.

Another blanket option available is a tail connection strap that holds the blanket in place across a horse's hindquarters. Some blankets also have leg straps that connect around the top of the legs.

Equine Tip

For colder conditions, there is a tail curtain, or tail skirt, attachment. It is usually a piece that fits over the tail to provide warmth and protection from wind and rain. On some blankets that have this piece, the curtain can be removed as temperatures warm up.

Most of the blankets used at stables where the horses get a lot of riding do not have a tail curtain. They are used more commonly on horses that are not as active.

Blanket Expenses

The cost of a horse blanket can range from $35 to nearly $300. The extra costs are for such things as special waterproof designs, ease and strength of connections, as well as for strong and reinforced materials that also provide comfort and protection from bumps and bites.

You can get rust-resistant buckles and other metal in the blankets. You might also pay more for more breathable fabric as well as a more expensive lining, which can help keep the horse's skin smooth.

There are some other additions you might want, like reflectors, something like what you put on your kid's shoes so cars can see them at night when they cross a street. For a horse, the reflectors just make them easier to spot in the field or paddock. (Presumably, the horse won't be out in traffic, at least not by himself.)

Horse Sense

If you're living in a colder climate, your horse will probably wear out his blankets fairly quickly during the winter. Constant use will put particular pressure on such areas as the blanket leg straps, which will get worn because of all the horse's movements.

If the blankets you're using have leg straps, they will likely have to be replaced. On many blankets, they are not detachable but are sewn right into the blanket. You can carefully remove the stitching if you know how, or you might just buy a new blanket.

Sheets

Sheets are generally lumped in with blankets, especially by companies that are selling horse equipment. The attachments for sheets are normally similar to those used on blankets, as are the costs. Sheets are generally lighter weight than blankets, made of cotton and nylon. Though they can be used to keep a horse warm, their more common use is to keep the horse dry during rain. They are light enough that they can also be kept on the horse during the summer to ward off insect bites.

Since sheets are usually lighter, there are other features that aren't usually found on heavier blankets. On some variations, sheets can be put on over the horse's head, like a person puts on a sweater. There are also sheets that can be stepped into with the front legs and then pulled up around the horse's chest and neck.

Sheets are also used for therapeutic reasons. The right material of sheet can add comfort to a horse who has back problems.

Coolers

Coolers are used to keep the horse dry after he has been worked out or bathed. They are put on the horse while he's being walked, or cooled out. The material is breathable. This lets the horse get dry without getting cold and prevents his body temperature from dropping too low.

Coolers, which are sometimes called mantles, are usually made of wool and cotton or similar synthetic material. Coolers seem to look like a cape because they are not tied as tightly as blankets or sheets. They also do not have as many attachments.

Usually, a cooler is fastened around the head with a browband that attaches under the ears. There is often a loose tie around the tail. Only in windy conditions is a belly strap or surcingle added.

Riding Vocab

Surcingle is a term used for the strap that goes under the horse to connect a blanket or a sheet. The term can also be used to describe a saddle connection, though the words girth and cinch are much more commonly used for those straps.

Sometimes a sheet, known as the anti-sweat sheet, is placed under the cooler. It's designed to absorb most of the moisture coming off the horse.

Hoods and Shoulder Guards

Hoods, also called fly masks, fit over the horse's head and look like a blindfold. However, the horse can see through most of these hoods. They are designed to shield the eyes from bright lights and protect them after surgery. They can also be used to keep flies, not to mention dirt, dust, and debris, away from the horse's face.

The best hoods attach under the jaw, usually with a double attachment.

Shoulder guards are designed for protection, particularly for horses who have skin irritations caused by blankets. They fit around the horse's shoulders and under his front legs. They are attached by a side release. Shoulder guards are usually made of nylon.

Trailering Your Horse

If you own a horse, you'll probably need to transport him. You might be traveling to shows or to competitions, but you may also need to go to a veterinarian. To do so, you'll need access to a trailer.

If you decide to buy a trailer, the first thing you need to do is figure out how often you're going to be using it. If you're not planning to travel frequently with your horse, you won't need to get the fanciest, newest model. You can get a fine used trailer for a cost much lower than the latest versions.

You also need to know how many horses you'll be transporting. If it's just one, you shouldn't buy anything bigger than a two-horse trailer. A large trailer also requires a larger vehicle to tow the trailer.

Another consideration is the purpose of your trailering. If you're going to be traveling to shows with your horse, you might need a trailer that has an area for you to dress in and maybe an area for you to sleep in.

Checking the Trailer

Checking a horse trailer before you purchase it is pretty much the same as checking a truck or utility vehicle. The same familiar items need to be inspected, including the chassis, springs, and suspension. But there are other items unique to trailers that have to be checked, including the reversing arm and jockey wheel.

Trailer Prices

The prices on horse trailers are pretty close to the prices of trucks or vans. You can buy a good used trailer for just a few thousand dollars, or you can spend more than $50,000 to buy the newest models with the best features. The most expensive models often include living quarters for the owner.

A fairly simple, new two-horse van should cost you about $10,000, though remember you also need a truck to haul it.

Renting a Trailer

You'll have a much more reasonable expense if you decide to rent a horse trailer. The expenses are not all that much more than renting a car, at least if you do some shopping on the Internet. You can probably rent a trailer for $200 a day or even less. If you're only transporting your horse once or twice a month, the renting option makes a lot more sense than the many thousands you'd pay to buy a trailer.

Leasing a Trailer

Much like leasing a car or any other vehicle, leasing is the best option for certain people who need to use a horse trailer. The payments tend to be lower than the monthly payments for buying. Usually, there is also no down payment required.

Getting Your Horse Inside

Getting into a trailer is not a natural activity for a horse at all, so there can be a number of issues. It may take a young horse a good while before he is comfortable getting into the vehicle. When you are buying an older horse and you're going to be traveling quite a bit with him, you should certainly make sure you can get him on a trailer safely before you purchase him.

Make sure you have enough room for the horse, or horses, in the trailers. The horse should have enough room to move all of his legs. There should be enough height and width in the trailer so the horse does not feel cramped. The best vans have enough room for the horses to turn around so they can be led out head first.

In addition to being able to move his legs, the horse needs to be able to move his head freely. He cannot feel restrained when he needs to clear out his breathing passages after dust or other particles get into his lungs.

Ventilation is also important for a horse in a trailer. The horse needs relief from the smells within the trailer, such as manure and urine. Good air circulation is also needed so he doesn't get too hot or too cold during his trip.

Ideally, all the horses in the van should be able to be unloaded individually. Make sure everything else about the trailer is safe, which means no sharp edges. The latches and other attachments must be strong and durable. The floors and sides also need to be secure.

Also make sure that the ramp used for getting on and off the trailer is set up securely. Make sure it is of adequate length and is not slippery. A nice extra feature for a van would be an extra entrance and exit.

Horse Sense

One of the main reasons that horses get frightened or spooked when getting into a trailer is the lack of light. Make sure that there is enough light in the van for the horse to see. Make sure you haven't parked the trailer in bright light, which would create a drastic change in brightness for the horse as he goes inside.

One last point is about your own safety. Make sure there is room for you to get around safely and to get off the van. Make sure you're not going to be trapped inside by an angry horse. Never forget the possible dangers around such large animals.

CHAPTER 20

 **Your Horse's Health**

> ## In This Chapter
> ➤ Food and digestions
> ➤ Breeding and development
> ➤ Choosing a vet and routine care
> ➤ Foot care

In this chapter, you'll learn about what your horse needs to eat and other health needs of your horse. You'll learn the steps you need to take when choosing a vet and the ways you can monitor your horse's health. You'll also learn how to manage emergencies. And you'll learn about farriers, the people who take care of horses' feet.

Horse Digestion

It's a rather long journey for the food that a horse eats. It goes down his throat, through his lungs, and down his long esophagus, which is at least 4 feet long, to his belly.

The stomach of the horse is rather small and not capable of absorbing a good deal of food. The stomach sits between the horse's liver, which is more forward and lower, and the spleen, which is just behind. The stomach is separated from the chest by the diaphragm. A horse has both a small and a large intestine, and a small and a large colon. The food passes through and out of his system in the expected way.

There can be serious problems if a horse is forced to exercise too quickly after eating. The horse needs about an hour to digest his food before he is ready for exercise. If he is rushed into moving quickly before that, stomach problems can develop, including colic. There is also a risk of other severe problems, such as the stomach becoming ruptured or the lungs becoming filled with blood.

Because of their small stomach, horses are designed to digest their food slowly. In the wild, horses eat small amounts of food all day, but that is not usually practical for a domesticated horse. The best arrangement for a horse in a barn is to feed him four times a day, with 4 pounds of food at each serving.

Horse Food

Horses' feed consists mostly of grains, grasses, and legumes. They should get about 70 percent of their food from those fiber-rich foods.

Grasses and Legumes

The grasses that horses graze on are many, usually divided by the season. Grasses that grow in cooler climates are generally more palatable for the horse, though, obviously, they don't grow everywhere. The most common legume in the horse's diet is alfalfa, usually given to him in cube form.

Equine Tip

Horses face a special danger from a couple of summer grasses. Make sure your horse is not grazing on Sudan grass or johnsongrass, both of which are known to be toxic to horses.

There are a number of grains that a horse eats, including rice, oats, corn, barley, wheat, and rye. Horse grains are usually fed to the horse on a tray on the floor.

Hay

Most of the time, domesticated horses are eating hay, which is the dried form of grasses or alfalfa. About 80 percent of hay is dried concentrate, as opposed to about 20 percent of the same food eaten during grazing. Because of the concentration of the food source, hay has a higher nutritional value than regular grasses.

Especially in winter months, when grasses are rare or nonexistent, dried hay makes up the bulk of a horse's diet. A horse will eat at least 20 pounds a day of hay when conditions prevent him from grazing.

Hay is sold in bales that weigh 40 pounds. The hay should be a bright color and should be clear of mold spores, which appear as white dust.

Hay is fed to a horse in his stall in a hay rack, which is placed slightly below the height of the horse's neck.

Supplements

Usually, a vitamin and mineral supplement is given to a horse, although most of the food purchased for a horse is already fortified. Horses that are more active need more calcium and other minerals, which can be provided by supplements.

Senior Horses

Older horses tend to have more trouble chewing and digesting their food. It's important if you have an elderly horse that you get him special hay and other foods that are easy to chew and digest. Feed manufacturers produce foods that are specially designed for the needs of elderly horses.

Horse Sense

Silage is an alternative to hay in colder climates where it is more difficult to dry the grasses and turn them into hay. Silage is the result of removing moisture from the grasses through fermentation. The practice is more common in Europe than it is in America.

Storing the Food

Hay needs to be kept in a dry, elevated, and well-ventilated location. Most farms have their own hay storage sheds, where the bales are stacked and stored.

Grain storage does not have to be that expensive. Cans that can hold up to 100 pounds of grain can be bought cheaply. Just make sure that they are waterproof and pest resistant.

Food Costs

As of early 2013, hay costs around $5 a bale. Remember that a horse eats half a bale a day. Grains are not as expensive, costing about $2.50.

The price of supplements can vary a great deal. A standard supplement costs about $15 a month, but more specialized supplements can cost $50 a month or more. Consult with your vet to see what supplements your horse should have.

Water

Water is even more important to the horse than food. A horse can sometimes survive for weeks without food, but he will die after just a few days without water. So make sure you always have a supply of it available.

A typical horse drinks and needs about 4 to 5 gallons of water a day.

Equine Tip

A horse is more in danger of becoming dehydrated in the cold winter than in the summer. With his small stomach, drinking cold water is painful for the horse. Usually, a horse will refuse to drink cold water, or won't drink enough of it, which can lead to dehydration.

A horse will eat it snow but won't get nearly enough liquid from it. Make sure your horse's water doesn't freeze. You might consider warming it, but be careful. If there's electrical wiring involved, make sure the horse does not get a shock.

Horse Breeding

By age three, horses are capable of breeding, though domesticated horses usually aren't mated until they are older. Mares often have foals beyond the age of twenty. Many stallions can still be potent over twenty as well, though they tend to be less fertile.

Horse Sense

On breeding farms, it's a standard procedure for the mare to have her legs tied during the mating session with the stallion. This is done for the safety of the stud, since mares are known to kick back with their legs, and many stallions have been injured.

Muzzles are often utilized on mares as well to keep them from biting the stallion. There may also be helmets placed on either one of the horses as a precaution against head injuries.

The planned mating of domesticated horses takes most of the romance out of it. Usually, the mare is brought into the barn after the handlers have made sure that she is ready. Then the stallion is led in. The whole process takes but a few minutes. This is apparently an inherited trait since the short mating session limits the time wild horses are in danger of attacks from predators.

Pregnancy

A mare is pregnant for eleven months, sometimes a little longer. Twin births are rare, and the foals often don't survive. Even if they do survive, twins are usually weak or small and not as strong as non-twins.

Riding Vocab

There are a lot of expressions used in breeding horses that may seem a little rude or less than tactful.

Covering a mare refers to the stallion being mated with a mare.

Stopping a mare means that the stallion got her pregnant.

Birth

When a mare is ready to give birth, she seeks an isolated location. For safety reasons, she also waits until the cover of night to give birth. Normally, she also seeks a damp area for the event.

The mare's water bursts, as the sac in which the foal has grown is severed. The foal then comes out feet first. Its eyes are wide open as he arrives.

After the foal has come out, the mother lays still for a while before rising up, as the umbilical cord needs to send the last bit of blood from the mother into the new foal. At the right time, she rises up, which cuts the cord.

The mare then greets her new baby with a soft vocal greeting that the foal will remember as his mother's call. Occasionally, a new foal will also respond with a sound. The mother then starts licking the foal clean for many minutes. In the process, she will absorb the scent of her offspring so she can identify him in the months to come.

Within half an hour after arriving, the new foal tries to stand up. This usually takes several attempts, but normally the foal makes it up to his feet within an hour. Soon after, he begins nursing.

Within a day, the newborn's senses and body functions are all working. He can run in the field and get into the strides of the horse's natural gaits.

Within a couple of weeks, the horse's baby teeth begin to appear. Soon after, the youngster begins interacting with other new foals. He is well on his way to becoming a social animal.

Yearlings and Weanlings

In the wild, a mother usually drives off her foal by the time she is ready to have another one. In domestic settings, at a specified age, the farm separates, or weans, the foals from their mothers. Young horses less than a year old that are no longer with their mother are known as weanlings.

Breaking a Horse

The process of getting horses used to being saddled and ridden is known as breaking a horse (in the sense of breaking them in.) The decision as to when this is done depends on the type of activity a horse is being raised for. Dressage horses, for example, tend to be developed at a later age, so there is no need to hurry the process. The same is true of polo ponies. But horses being raised to race under saddle, such as Thoroughbreds, need to be broken and ready to be ridden before they turn two.

The old theories of breaking horses tended to be along the line of repetition. The process of getting the horse to stand still and accept a saddle and a rider was repeated many times until the horse grudgingly went along. Now the process has become more psychological, with the handlers using the instincts of the horses to help get them to accept these new demands.

Even with the new, gentler approaches, it takes a great deal of patience and understanding to get a horse properly broken. The first person to get on a horse's back can expect to be thrown off many times during the process. That's why the breaking usually takes places in a ring or paddock that includes a good deal of soft material to ease the falls and throws.

Ready to Go

Once a horse has been broken, he is then moved on to his next location, be it a ranch or a training center, where he will be trained at whatever his intended activity might be.

A Horse's Life

There is no simple way of comparing a horse's age and life span to that of a human's, but the closest equivalent would be 1 horse year for every 5 human years. This works pretty well for horses from about age 3 to 12, but before and after those ages, the numbers need to be adjusted. A 2-year-old colt (male) or filly (female) is more mature than a human 10-year-old.

Horses can and do live to age 30 and somewhat beyond. These old equines are not the equivalent of 150-year-old humans, who obviously don't exist. They are more like the geriatric humans, age 80 or 90. Like their human counterparts, the senior horses get gray hairs and wrinkles and find it more difficult to get around.

Choosing a Vet

A horse can't live into old age without good health care. When choosing a veterinarian for your horse or barn, make sure he is a specialist in large animals. The person who treats your dog or cat a couple of times a year may be legally qualified to treat horses, but he may not do much, if any, work with horses and is probably not up on the latest medicines and treatment procedures.

You also want a vet who is close enough to your horse's location so that he can get there in an emergency. Many vets do go to farms to treat horses, so it may not be necessary for you to go to your vet's office. This is convenient, but it is likely to cost more.

If you aren't sure what vet to use, as with most horse matters, you can ask more experienced horse and barn owners for advice.

Vet Expenses

Your veterinarian bills will obviously depend on the health of your horse. If there is a need for major surgery, the expenses can run into several thousands of dollars. But if your horse is reasonably healthy and just needs standard care such as immunizations, the annual bill will be about $300.

Riding Vocab

Rasping the teeth of a horse is also known as floating the teeth. The name comes from the file that is used for the procedure, which someone thought resembled the shape of a boat.

Routine Visits

Even if he's healthy, your horse will need to see a vet at certain times for routine procedures. The vet will give the horse his required vaccinations and a checkup, including a check of the teeth. Though there are horse doctors who work specifically as dentists, a regular vet can rasp the teeth to keep them smooth and pain-free. This procedure is necessary at least a few times a year since a horse's teeth are continually growing.

Worming

Worming is a procedure designed to prevent a horse from being infested by of all kinds of parasites, be they worms or otherwise. The parasites get into the horse's stomach and damage the intestines among other interior parts.

Horses are not able to vomit, so it is difficult for them to correct any problem that develops in their digestive systems.

Worming is usually done every two to three months and is now usually administered as an oral injection.

The protection of your horse from parasites requires more than just worming. Good prevention also comes from keeping the horse's stall clean, separating out the good from the bad straw, and proper disposal of the remains.

Do It Yourself

Major issues such as bleeding or lameness require a vet, but there are a number of things you can do safely on your own. One thing you can do for sure is take the horse's vital signs.

The Pulse

You can take a horse's pulse about the same way you would take a human pulse. There are several places you can find his pulse, including under the jaw and over the eye. A normal pulse for a horse is between 30 and 45 beats.

Respiration

A horse should be taking anywhere from eight to fourteen breaths a minute. If you can't find a way to count your horse's breaths, you can hold a mirror in front of his nose and count the number of times the mirror becomes steamed by his breath.

Temperature

A normal horse temperature is 100.4 degrees, though some horses, such as pregnant mares, may have a higher temperature.

The thermometers are all rectal, so you'll have to learn how to insert them. Normally you will lubricate the thermometer, as well as the horse's rectal opening before you insert the thermometer.

Follow the manufacturer's instructions as to how much time is needed to get the temperature and how much time is needed before the thermometer gives you the proper reading.

Don't forget to disinfect the thermometer afterward, washing it in warm water with soap. Then allow it to dry for over an hour before storing.

First Aid

It's important to have a first aid kit for your horse. Call in your vet for serious cuts and abrasions, but you can treat minor scrapes with a thorough cleaning. You should have iodine and an antibiotic ointment on hand to use as a wound cleanser and antiseptic.

An antibiotic ointment, much as with humans, will help protect an injury from infection. There are also wound powders that are used for the same purpose.

You'll need to have other medical aids on hand to handle slight problems. These include leg wraps and bandages. You should also have sponges available as well as clean rags.

Be Careful of the Doses!

It's easy to make a mental error on doses. You may be giving your horse a few different routine medical pills or doses and it's possible you might get confused or have what is sometimes known as a brain cramp. This can obviously be quite dangerous if you're giving your horse some kind of pain reliever or other small dose. If you've given out the wrong dose on something, just get help right away. Normally, the overdose can be dealt with, as long as you deal with it quickly.

Nonroutine Visits

Your horse can have a number of serious conditions that require a vet's attention. In many cases, you may not know what the problem is, but the horse's actions are unusual and indicate that something is wrong.

The Horse is Acting Strange

He may be pacing in his stall, he may be rolling on the ground or he could be staring at his side. These are all signs of a problem. Something feels strange to him and the horse is trying to find some way to relieve his discomfort.

There is an Unusual Nasal Discharge

Horses usually have a slightly watery discharge from the nose after exertion, but if it's too heavy or if it contains blood, there's a problem. Also, check the color. If the discharge is yellow or green, that is a sign of infection and medical attention is needed.

Horse Sense

Unlike cats, horses are not finicky eaters. They like to eat—all day if possible—and they need to eat a lot. Normally, their small stomach hurts if it is empty. So if your horse is not eating (the term is going off his feed), there is usually a problem; Something is going on that is making it painful for the horse to swallow or digest. You need to call the vet if this happens.

Other Serious Problems

A horse's eyes should not be swollen, red, or discharging heavy fluid. The skin should be bright, and there should be no signs of spots or swelling. There should also be no bare patches of hair on the horse's coat.

Look out for cold sweating. This is not at all normal for a horse and is a possible sign of shock.

Dehydration is also a serious problem. The most common test to check a horse for dehydration is to open the horse's mouth. Put your finger on his gum for a couple of seconds. If the color does not return to the spot quickly, the horse is either dehydrated or losing blood.

Horses can get the equine equivalent of diarrhea. Normally, they should be relieving themselves every couple of hours. In addition to the frequency, you should also check that there is no blood in the stools or unusual coloring.

Other problems that require a call to the vet just take common sense to detect. If a horse is walking in pain or not putting weight on a foot, if there is a sign of major blood loss or the presence of a large abscess, you should know enough to get help quickly.

Laminitis

Perhaps the most serious and most likely fatal disease a horse can encounter is laminitis. Also known as founder, laminitis is an inflammation of part of the foot that can cause lameness and result in severe pain. Certain diets too high in sugar can also contribute to the development of laminitis.

Eventually, most horses with laminitis are in such obvious pain that they are euthanized to prevent further suffering.

Equine Tip

Laminitis can be a particular problem in a four-season climate. The first grasses growing in spring are often quite high in sugar content, more than a horse needs. The extra sugar can lead to the disease.

If you live in such a climate, be careful how much grass you let your horse eat in the spring, especially if he has issues with his feet. The high sugar content can also lead to problems with colic.

Colic

Colic is a problem that also affects humans, in particular young children, but it's potentially much more dangerous and deadly in horses. Almost any digestive problems could be a sign that a horse has colic.

Normally, the disease is caused by excessive gas in the gastro-intestinal tract, which can result in a complete blockage of the tract. A horse shows signs of colic if he is unusually restless, going up and down quite a bit. It is his attempt to relieve his pain.

Dehydration is a leading cause of colic, as is parasite infestation. A lack of water can lead to blockages in the intestines as the horse will not have enough fluid to clear its system.

The intestines can also become twisted and virtually tied up. This is known as torsion colic.

A vet cannot resolve a case of colic until he knows which version of the disease he is dealing with.

One of the best ways to prevent your horse from getting the disease is to make sure you're providing him with all the parasite prevention he needs. Also make sure that he is drinking enough water. Try to make sure the temperature of the water is not too cold or the horse won't drink it.

Choosing a Farrier

Since the well-being of the feet of your horse is so important, the choice of a farrier is vital. This is the person who will take care of your horse's hooves as well as decide on the proper shoes. He will also make the shoes and put them on.

If you're boarding your horse at a stable, it likely has its own farrier who can take care of your horse. But you'll want to meet him and talk to him. In fact, the quality of the farrier may be one of the deciding factors when you're deciding where to board your horse.

Even if you're going to hire your own farrier, you'll probably be relying on the advice of others before you make a selection. But, as with anyone else you hire, you do want to ask him some questions first. Find out about his experience with the type of horse that you have. A farrier may well be familiar with certain breeds and certain activities, but maybe not the kind you want. If you have a pony, find a farrier who's familiar with them.

Riding Vocab

The job of a farrier is to treat the feet and design and make the shoes for horses as well as other farm animals. A blacksmith is someone who works with metal and iron. However, in some regions of the country, there can be confusion, since a farrier is also referred to as a blacksmith.

If you choose a vet before you choose a farrier, you can ask your vet to recommend someone (of course, if you pick a farrier first, you can ask him to recommend a vet).

Just as with a vet, you'll want the farrier to be close enough to your horse to get to him if there's an emergency.

Farrier Costs

The monthly expenses for caring for your horse's feet should be somewhere around $25. Putting on new shoes adds to the expense. For each new set of shoes, the farrier will charge about $80.

 # Owning Your Own Barn

In This Chapter

➤ Legal requirements

➤ Insurance and other requirements

➤ Barn features

➤ The joys of riding

In this chapter, you'll learn what you need to do if you decide to buy your own barn. You'll learn about the legal requirements and the insurance that you'll need. And you'll learn about the facility, itself, and how you need to maintain it.

The Laws

If you're buying a barn that's already in use, do not assume that it's legal for you to run it. The previous owner may have been in violation of community laws or may have had a special dispensation not available to you. Before you take the big step of buying a property, always find out first that it's legal for you to operate it.

If you already own a property and you want to keep a horse on it, you might not be allowed to. Even if you think you have enough room, the zoning laws may require you to have more.

Even if you have enough room, there may be other rules that prohibit horses from being kept in the community. In many places, horses are considered to be dangerous and prone to causing damage. There are also other issues that cause objections, like manure pits. If you are allowed to own a horse, make sure you know the rules about disposal of manure and bedding, among other things.

Once you know that you will not have any problem with the regulations or zoning laws, than get all the licensing you require both to run a barn and to board other people's horses.

Hire a lawyer to help you and make sure he is familiar with equine law. In the horse environment you've now embraced, there shouldn't be any problem getting the name of someone reliable.

Commercial Insurance

Since you're going to own horses that will be ridden by others on your farm, you'll need to get commercial equine liability insurance. Depending on the size of your facility, you can probably get all the coverage you need for somewhere between $100 and $200 a month. This should give you full coverage on all the activities and properties you own and run at your facility.

Insurance Demands

Your insurance company will require your facility to have several central requirements such as locked and monitored gates. It is likely to require you to post signs around the property such as Keep Out and Private Property. Such signs will lessen liability payments should an intruder be injured on your grounds.

You'll also be required to have other security features around the stable, including locks and special lighting.

Contracts

If you're going to own a barn and board other people's horses, you'll need to have a basic contract for your service explaining all you offer and don't offer. You must tell the prospective client such things as whether you're going to provide the horse's feed or whether the owner will have to pay for it. You'll also have to specify the food you're using as well as the bedding and other items you'll be using such as liniments and shampoos.

The contract should also specify how much exercising the horse will get and detail your insurance coverage—what's covered and what isn't.

The length of the contract needs to be specified, as well as the date and amount of payments.

Barn Requirements

When choosing a barn for purchase, you need to check a number of factors to make sure that they are up to standard. Perhaps most important is ventilation. This is important to keep the horses (and people) cool, but it is also important for controlling viruses and germs. When you enter the barn area, it should feel about as ventilated as the outdoors, or at least there shouldn't seem to be a drastic difference.

Drainage is also very important, not just around the stalls but inside them. Drainage of urine through the bottom of the stall is a big help.

You also have to make sure that all of the water pipes and electrical wiring is encased and not exposed to contact with the horses. Of course you'll also need to make sure all the basic safety requirements are up to date, such as checking smoke alarm batteries and testing fire extinguishers and their placement.

The Stalls

A stall should be in the shape of a square, with enough room for a horse to lie down comfortably. The largest stalls are about 18 × 18 feet, though most horses don't need that much room. Ponies can be quite comfortable in a stall that is 10 × 10 feet. If you have a full-sized horse, the roof of the stall needs to be at least 10, preferably 11, feet high.

Horses usually like to rub up against the side wood panels of their stalls, so there is no need for anything fancier. Painted sides can be dangerous if the horse ingests them.

Ideally, a stall should also have a window for the horse to look out. There should also be an opening in the door in which the horse can stick out both his head and neck. A horse is a social animal and appreciates seeing and communicating with other horses in the barn.

Horse Sense

Horses are such a social animal that not only do they become friendly with other horses but also with other creatures. It's quite common for a stable of horses to have cats and dogs around as well as some farm animals, usually goats.

Horses often become quite attached to these other species, and the cats, dogs, and goats can become attached to the horses and be quite protective of them.

A horse should have easy access to his water and food, but neither should be in a location that might cause injury.

The bedding on the floor of a stall needs to be cleaned, or mucked out, and replaced at least once a day. A large facility has a specific location for a manure pit for the disposal of used bedding.

Riding Vocab

Tack is short for tackle, meaning the equipment used. It's the same as the term used in fishing, as in bait and tackle.

The Tack Room

A major part of any barn is the tack room. It is where all the horse gear, as well as the oil, soap, and whatever else is needed, is kept and stored.

Some tack rooms may include washers and dryers for such items as blankets and sheets as well as riders' clothes. All the medical supplies can also be stored in the tack room as well. You may provide each owner with his own area in the tack room, including storage bins.

Make sure the tack room has adequate and safe electrical outlets. You don't want a tack room—or for that matter, any part of the facility—to have several stretched-out extension cords that could increase the risk of fire.

Since the equipment in the tack room, even just the parts used by the horses, is worth thousands of dollars, make sure your insurance covers you for theft, fire, natural disasters, and whatever other ways the items kept in the tack room can be lost or stolen.

Equine Tip

Depending on the climate you're in, the tack room may need to have both air conditioning and heating. Extreme temperatures in either direction can result in problems for much of the equipment being used, especially the leather goods.

Very hot or very cold conditions of course can also affect the people who go into the tack room. Also remember that in any climate, the tack room will need good ventilation.

The Paddock

Horses need to be turned out of the stalls every day for exercise and their mental well-being. Staying inside a stall all day is not a natural state for horses, so it's important that they be given the chance to roam around a paddock.

The paddocks to be used by the horses need to be well-kept grassy fields. Horses need to lie down and roll around on the ground, so the grass needs to be adequate for these actions. The grass not only needs to be well kept, but it also has to have good drainage.

With the exception of some male stallions, horses enjoy the company of other horses in their paddock or at least in adjoining paddocks, where they can meet.

Horse Sense

At some race tracks, hedges are used to mark off paths and turns instead of the usual wooden rails. Horses are known to run very close to a hedge, even rubbing against it. They will not run as close to a wooden rail.

Fencing and Hedges

When horses are outside, they need to be in an enclosed area, so the fencing on the farm is important. This includes the natural fencing of hedges. They need to be wide and thick and high enough to keep a horse from jumping over them. They cannot be made of any growth so prickly that a horse could get injured. Horses seem to enjoy being around hedges, which are also good for the environment.

Fences are usually made of wire or, more expensively, traditional wooden railings. Wooden rails are often painted a bright color, usually white, which stands out against the green grass.

Horse Sense

When the world-famous Calumet Farm had to be sold in 1992, the residents around the facility in Lexington, Kentucky, were quite worried because one of the prospective bidders promised to do away with the traditional and famous white fencing of the farm. He planned to install different, more economical fencing. But the winning bidder, Henryk DeKwiatkowski, a Polish industrialist and World War II Royal Air Force hero, was the winning bidder, and his first announcement after the auction was that the fences would be "painted white as long as I live." This was immediately greeted by an audible cheer from the local residents.

However, white fences, though beautifully ornamental, make little difference to the horses. Though they are not color blind, they have no particular reaction to white fencing, other than they can differentiate it from the green grass.

The Joys of Riding

Once you've stepped into the world of horses, you'll find yourself in the company of like-minded people—your fellow riders. All of you enjoy the pleasures of being on a horse's back and welcome the chance to get to know and handle your horses.

Horse people love animals, and they care about their well-being. They enjoy the same challenges that you do. Even if you're interested in dressage and your new friends are barrel racers, even if you have a Thoroughbred and they have ponies, you're all still riders with a love of horses.

Sport for the Whole Family

The fact that horse people are good people is one reason that you'll want to get your children involved. If they become enthusiastic about riding, they can pursue this activity throughout their lives.

When your children get involved with riding, you'll notice their excitement. They'll want to learn everything about riding as quickly as they can. They'll be making friends with fellow horse enthusiasts, and they'll be developing a sense of responsibility as they care for the horses.

The Pleasures of Riding

For all the work your horse might do and for all the competitions he might compete in, you should never forget the simple pleasure that your horse can give you. The connection is similar to any that you might have with a pet, but it can be even greater.

Riding a horse is truly the closest connection possible between human and animal. You're moving together, you're observing things at the same time, and you're experiencing excitement and exhilaration simultaneously.

Horses and riders can develop a real kinship. The horse likes it when you give him praise, and you like making him happy with your words and gestures. You and your horse can develop a special feeling of compatibility. Other people may handle your horse and other people may ride your horse, but you two can develop a special feeling of friendship.

The time spent with your horse will make your life more enjoyable. You will look forward to the ride. You will enjoy your time together. Whatever problems there may be in your life will seem more palatable when you're around your horse.

The more time you spend with horses, the more you will like them. Despite their size, their instincts and desire for fun and pleasure are similar to yours. What's more, they show it with a great deal of regality.

Being on a horse's back while he is striding powerfully is truly a sublime experience. You feel in touch with the horse's strength and his grace. The strides of a horse, be it the slow walk, the controlled trot, the canter, or the full-out gallop, show off the horse's unique characteristics. There is no other animal that can provide you with such a feeling.

The majestic qualities of horses are unique. They have played a major part in the lives of the human race for over 5,000 years. May they continue to be a big part of our lives forever.

CHAPTER 22

Horse Racing

In This Chapter

➤ Owning a race horse

➤ Breeding a race horse

➤ Becoming a trainer or jockey

In this chapter, you will learn about the ways you can become a part of the horse racing industry. You'll learn how you can get involved whether you want the occasional thrill of watching one or two of your own horses compete, or whether you want to own, breed or train a large stable. You'll also learn how you can become a rider of race horses.

Getting Involved

Horse racing is a multi-billion dollar industry which is conducted on five continents. You could become a part of the sport whether you want to spend just a few thousand dollars or many, many millions.

These days, horses race at all times of the year. The most high-profile racing takes place in or near the major cities of the world and usually involves either Thoroughbreds or those breeds closely related to the Thoroughbred, including the Standardbred, the Quarter Horse and the Arabian.

Unlike equestrian and hunt racing, the horse racing which takes place at racetracks is fueled by gambling dollars. A percentage of all money bet on each race is set aside to fund cash prizes, known as "purse money."

By far the biggest portion of the industry is Thoroughbred racing. The most popular centers of the sport are in the United Kingdom, France, Germany, Hong Kong, Japan, Australia and the United States, though it is also quite popular in many other countries. The major centers of racing are also the main centers of horse breeding, with Ireland, Japan, the United States and Australia being dominant early in the twenty-first century.

In the United States, the state of Kentucky, with it's famous lush blue grasses, is by far the leading state producing racing horses. But virtually everywhere there is racing, there is also breeding.

Owning a Race Horse

Whatever type of racing horse you want, there are many ways for you to get involved. You could breed your own, but you also could buy horses at auction. No matter which breed you are interested in, you can find a major sale of potential race horses. They are sold as weanlings, yearlings and two year olds.

Horses do not race until age two. If you buy them at a younger age than that, the price you pay is based strictly on potential. The value of yearlings and weanlings is determined by their breeding and their conformation.

Equine Tip

Another way that many horse owners and traders make money in the industry is through re-selling young horses. They buy a yearling or a weanling for a low amount on the assumption that the horse will become more physically imposing when he gets older and that he will run fast when he enters training. If the horse does mature as they hope, they can re-sell the horse as a two year old for a higher price than they paid. This practice is known as "Pinhooking."

Sales of two year olds tend to be a different matter. Those horses have already begun training at a racetrack. Their sales prices are not only based on breeding and conformation, but also on how fast they can run.

The prices paid for these young horses vary widely. The best bred, best looking yearlings and weanlings sell for millions of dollars and so do the fastest two year olds. But it is also possible to find good race horses at auctions for just a few thousand dollars. Keep in mind that there have been some very expensive horses that have never won a race while some very inexpensive horses have gone on to become champions.

Horses in Training

You don't have to buy horses before they race. You can buy them in events known as "claiming races." Any licensed owner can put in a claim for any horse in such a race. Every horse entered has a listed claiming, or sale price.

If you want to buy a horse in one of these races, you must enter a claim before they run. If you were the only one who entered a claim, the horse is yours as soon as the race is over.

Joining A Syndicate

You don't have to own a race horse by yourself. You can have one partner, two partners or as many as you want. Many racing stables specialize in offering opportunities for new owners to become involved in a syndicate. You can invest as much money as you choose.

For many syndicates, the fee you pay to own a horse will cover all expenses. Your share will give you full status as an owner and you will be able to enjoy all the privileges offered to this exclusive group.

Usually, the members of these syndicates do not have to worry about picking out the horse or the trainer. All of that is handled by the syndicate managers.

Syndicates continue to grow in popularity in most areas of the racing world. It's easy enough to find a syndicate since many of them advertise in the major industry publications.

Getting Good Advice

The horse racing industry is always looking for new horse owners and many racetracks offer seminars and other venues for anyone interested in becoming an owner. The seminars will explain the risks and benefits to you as an owner and they also provide information on how you can get involved in the sport.

Breeding Horses

Breeding race horses has always been considered an inexact science. "Breed the best to the best and hope for the best" is the most famous phrase that describes the process of breeding race horses.

There are many different ways you can get involved in horse racing breeding. You could buy broodmares and breed your own horses. When they are old enough, you can race them yourself or you can offer them for sale at auction.

You can also own shares in a stud horse. You could have the stallion mate with your mares, or you can sell the breeding rights to others.

You could also buy a breeding farm. Since most of these farms require a lot of space and a lot of help, this is the most expensive way to get involved in the breeding industry.

Owning Broodmares

Generally, broodmares are valued in three ways. If the mare has already produced foals that have raced, her value will be enhanced or diminished based on the performance of her offspring. If she has yet to produce a foal that has raced, she can be very valuable if she showed a great deal of ability as a race horse. Even if the mare didn't have an outstanding race record, or even if she never raced, she can still be valuable if her breeding is outstanding.

If you own a broodmare, you'll need to choose an appropriate stallion for her mating. If you also own a stud horse, or a share in a stud horse, your decision might be easy (although you'll want to make sure there is not too much inbreeding in the potential foal.)

Equine Tip

In most breeds, females are known as fillies until they are five, when they are then known as mares. But if a filly is bred at a young age, she will be listed as a mare even if she is only three or four years old.

If you do not own a stallion or a share in a stallion, you'll need to find one to breed to your mare. You'll have to determine how much you want to spend on a stud fee. You'll want a stallion whose fee is appropriate for the worth of your broodmare.

If you have a mare that is only considered to be worth a small amount, you probably won't be allowed to breed her to an expensive stallion even if you are willing to pay a large fee.

Owners of expensive stallions are quite worried about the quality of the foals that their stud will sire, so they want the mares mated to him to be of as high a quality as possible. In most cases, they can refuse a mare they consider to be unworthy of their stallion's value.

Stud Horses

Whatever racing breed you are involved with, the most valuable horses of all are the breeding stallions, or the potential breeding stallions. These days, many top stud horses are bred to over 100 mares a year. This makes them very valuable, since the owner of a stallion receives a fee for every foal that he sires.

While running at the race track, a top horse might be able to earn several million dollars in a year. But the amount of money that same horse can generate at stud is much greater. The top stallions in the world have stud fees well over $100,000. That means every foal that they sire will net the owner or owners of a stallion that much money in fees. When you multiply that total by over 100 foals a year, you get an idea of the huge amount of money that these horses are worth.

Equine Tip

When a mare is bred to a stud horse, the payments made to the stallion owner by the owner of the mare is usually contingent on a live foal being produced. The usual language of the contract describes the fee as payable "when the foal stands and nurses."

Of course, not many stallions command those types of fees and you can find a decent stallion for quite a bit less than that. The winner of the Kentucky Derby in 2014, California Chrome, was sired by a stallion named Lucky Pulpit whose stud fee was just $2,500.

After the success of California Chrome, the owners of Lucky Pulpit announced they would be raising his stud fee to $12,500 the next year. This is one of the ways that owners of stallions can make money. If you own a stallion or buy a share in a stallion, the value of those shares will grow dramatically if the offspring of the sire prove successful.

Horse Sense

In the northern hemisphere, the breeding season lasts from February until July. In the southern hemisphere, the breeding season is from August until January.

Once the northern hemisphere breeding has concluded, some stallions are then shipped to farms in the southern hemisphere where they have another full season at stud. This doubles the number of foals and doubles the value of the horse. This practice is usually only done with the most expensive stallions.

Stallion Syndicates

Stallion syndicates offer a lifetime breeding right to anyone who purchases a share in a stud horse. You can use your share to breed your own mare to the stallion, or you can sell the breeding right to someone else.

Riding Vocab

Some of the terms used in connection with race horse stallions are unique. The horse is said to be "Standing" at the location where he is performing his stud duties. The group of mares that he is mated with in a year are referred to as his "Book." If you own one breeding right to a stallion in a year, it is known as a "season."

Running A Stud Farm

A horse breeding farm is usually a very big and busy place. The top farms sometimes have 20-30 stallions at stud. They also have many mares at the farm to be bred to these stallions.

Many of these types of farms have hundreds and even thousands of acres to house the stallions, mares and foals. Obviously, if you haven't inherited such a place, it would cost you many millions to buy it.

However, there are also smaller breeding operations that do not require an overwhelming amount of money to purchase. There are farms that stand just one or two stallions and have a much smaller amount of area to house the studs and the mares.

High Financial Risks and Possible Great Rewards

All investments in race horses have the potential to make a great deal of money, but they all also offer the possibility of financial peril. If you want to race a horse, keep in mind that the stable fees that your trainer requires are about $3,000 a month. That total includes care, food, farriers and vet bills. That is more than almost any other horse will cost you.

The frustrations of owning or breeding race horses can be great, but there is also the chance you could be successful beyond what you might have hoped for. The best advice for those who want to get involved in horse racing is to make sure you can afford it. If you can discover a level of expense that you can handle, you could find it a very exciting and enjoyable way to spend your money.

Becoming A Trainer

There are many different paths taken by those who have become trainers of race horses. Many worked with horses in other capacities before they began to train.

There are several examples of veterinarians who switched careers and began to train. There are also many former riders who became trainers once their riding careers ended. It's also common to see someone who was involved in training other types of horses, such as jumpers and hunters, switch to race horses.

Still others became trainers by working their way up from less glamorous stable jobs such as groom or hot walker. Eventually they became stable foreman or an assistant trainer before they went out on their own.

Training Horses

The trainer is the person who manages the daily activities of a racing stable. He is in charge of keeping his horses ready to race, but there is much more to the job. He also has to select farriers, veterinarians and food suppliers for his stable. He also has to hire the help he needs for work around the barn.

Before a trainer can do any of those things, he must first find owners who will let him train their horses. Once he actually gets horses into his barn, he has to get them fit and then find the proper races for them.

If a trainer is successful, his owners will receive enough purse money to handle at least most of their costs. The owners may be encouraged enough to expand their stable and add more horses.

If the trainer continues to be successful, he may also attract other owners with other horses. The top trainers in the United States and Europe have as many as 200 horses in their barns. They receive ten percent of their stable's earnings. Several earn more than two million dollars a year.

Riding Race Horses

Traditionally, riders of race horses, known as jockeys, usually start at a young age when they are quite small. The amount of weight carried by race horses, including the rider, is light, usually well below 130 pounds. Anyone seeking a career as a professional jockey must first meet the size requirement. Almost no one begins a career as a jockey if they are more than 110 pounds.

Equine Tip

The terms used to describe the status of a jockey's career are the same as those used in other trades. When a jockey begins riding, he is known as an apprentice. When his time as an apprentice has ended and he becomes a full-time professional, he is then known as a journeyman.

Whatever country or region you are in, jockeys tend to begin their careers around farms or stables. Usually, they are first given work around the barn. Soon, they are given a chance to ride. If they begin to show promise as riders, they will be given more chances to exercise horses.

The prospective jockeys that are good enough will eventually be given a chance to ride in races. From that point, their riding talent will determine how far their careers will go.

Other Ways To Become A Jockey

Working around a stable is not the only way you can learn to become a jockey. There are also locations which offer training for jockeys to learn their profession. They are taught the refinements of how to sit and steer a race horse, as well as strategies to employ and other types of advice.

This type of training for jockeys has existed for many decades in the country of Panama. Their riding academy produced many of the great jockeys of the world. Such schools are now available in the United States as well. The most prominent one is located in the state of Kentucky and is directed by a former champion jockey, Chris McCarron.

Female Jockeys

In the United States, there were no female jockeys at all until the 1960s. In many other countries around the world, the profession was male-only for many more years after that. Until the sixties, female riders were banned from competing against male jockeys at all US race tracks. Even when the ban was lifted, many of the male jockeys at first refused to ride in races with females.

Riding Vocab

Before female jockeys became an accepted part of horse racing, among the many slang terms used for jockeys was boy. The most common use of the word came when a horse did not yet have a jockey announced. That horse was almost always listed as having "No Boy."

With the advent of female jockeys, that phrase gradually disappeared and has been replaced by the more generic "No Rider."

Eventually that all changed and though there are still more male jockeys, there are now many female jockeys who race with success and distinction against men at race courses around the world.

The Dangers of Race Riding

Generally, jockeys receive ten percent of the earnings of the horse they are riding (though if their mount earns no money, they are still paid a small fee.) With some races being worth hundreds of thousands and others worth millions of dollars, the top jockeys all earn a great deal of money in a year. However, the fragile nature of race horses makes this a very dangerous way to make a living. Jockeys have been killed during races and more have been paralyzed.

Perhaps the most famous horse of modern times, Secretariat, was ridden in most of his major successes by a highly successful Canadian jockey, Ron Turcotte. Unfortunately, just a few years after his great triumphs with that horse, Turcotte was thrown from a horse during a race in New York. He injured his spine so badly that he has been confined to a wheelchair for the rest of his life.

For many jockeys, the fear of this kind of injury is worse than the fear of death. Another great jockey, Angel Cordero Jr., said he wasn't afraid of being killed, he was more afraid of being paralyzed.

Even jockeys who do not suffer such catastrophic injuries are still subject to much damage when they fall off their horse. Another champion jockey, Laffit Pincay Jr., suffered a broken collarbone 21 times during his career.

Though there is always the threat of injuries when you are riding horses, the dangers are much greater for those who are riding in races for a living. The horses in these events are at a greater risk of injury because they are going faster than other horses. They are also bunched together when they are racing. If a jockey is thrown from a horse, he could be injured by the fall or he could be trampled by another horse.

Great rewards are possible for those who become jockeys, but you also have to consider the risks when you or your children decide to enter such a profession.

ABOUT THE AUTHOR

A horse enthusiast since childhood, Dean Server is also the author of four other books as well as numerous magazine articles on both horses and riders.

Mr. Server has a Master's Degree from California State University, Los Angeles. In addition to his writing career, Mr. Server is a teacher of English. He has taught in the public schools of both Trenton and Asbury Park, New Jersey.

An ardent support of animal shelters, Mr. Server is also a strong advocate and contributor to various other animal charities and nature projects.

Mr.Server currently resides in Ocean County, New Jersey.

INDEX

Made in the USA
San Bernardino, CA
17 October 2014